THE ORIGIN OF THE BUDDHA IMAGE

1—*Typical Buddha Figure. Anurādhapura. C. IV Cent. A. D.*

THE ORIGIN OF THE BUDDHA IMAGE

ANANDA K. COOMARASWAMY

MANOHAR
2024

First published 1927
Reprinted 2024

ISBN 978-81-19139-64-4

Published by
Ajay Kumar Jain *for*
Manohar Publishers & Distributors
4753/23 Ansari Road, Daryaganj
New Delhi 110 002

Printed at
Replika Press Pvt. Ltd.

THE ORIGIN OF THE BUDDHA IMAGE*

BY ANANDA K. COOMARASWAMY

"Nothing beyond what is self-developed in the brain of a race is permanently gained, or will survive the changes of time."

—FLINDERS PETRIE, in *Social Life in Ancient Egypt*

INTRODUCTION

THE question of the origin of the Buddha image is, of course, but a part of the general problem of the origin of Indian iconography and plastic types. In view of the thoroughly Indian character of mediaeval works it was natural in the first place to suppose that these types had been created and developed on Indian soil, and by Indian sculptors. This might well have seemed most obvious in the case of the Buddha figure, representing as it does, a conception of spiritual attainment altogether foreign to European psychology, and a formula quite un-European in its indifference to natural fact.

But it was soon realized, on the one hand, that the Buddha (Gautama, Śākya-Muni), in early Indian art, say before the first century A. D., is never represented in human form but only by symbols; and, on the other hand, that the Graeco-Buddhist or Indo-Hellenistic art of Gandhāra in the period immediately following presents us with an innumerable series of anthropomorphic images, certainly with some peculiarities of their own, but resembling in a general way the later Gupta and mediaeval images of India proper, not to speak of those of Farther India and the Far East. At once it was taken for granted that the idea of making such images had been suggested to the Indian mind from this outside source, and that Greek or at any rate Eurasian craftsmen had created the first images of the Buddha for Indian patrons on the foundation of a Hellenistic Apollo; and that the later images were not so much Indian as Indianized versions of the Hellenistic or, as it was more loosely expressed, Greek prototypes. This view was put forward, as M. Foucher himself admits, in a manner best calculated to flatter the prejudices of European students and to offend the susceptibilities of Indians: the creative genius of Greece had provided a model which had later been barbarized and degraded by races devoid of true artistic instincts, to whom nothing deserving the name of fine art could be credited.

From the standpoint of orthodox European scholarship the question was regarded as settled, and all that remained was to work out the details, a study which was undertaken by the founder of the theory in his already classic *L'art gréco-bouddhique du Gandhara*, and continued by Grünwedel and others, with this result at least, that the art of Gandhāra is now very thoroughly known. When, a little later, doubts were expressed from various quarters external to the circle of orthodox scholarship, doubts suggested rather by stylistic and *a priori* psychological considerations, than by purely archaeological evidence, M. Foucher, the author most committed to the Greek theory, did not hesitate to suggest in

*In order to get a large amount of comparative material together on the plates, short and incomplete captions have been printed there. A fuller record of the illustrations will be found in the list appended to the article.

his genial way that in the case of European students, these doubts were only the result of aesthetic prejudice, in the case of Indian students, of nationalist rancour (*"engouement d'aesthéticien ou rancune de nationaliste"*).[1]

Times have changed. I cannot better indicate the nature of this change than by a quotation from Mr. Dalton's recent work on *East Christian Art:* "The principles governing this Christian art have received their due; that which the eighteenth and nineteenth centuries refused to consider has been regarded with favouring eyes. Thus aid has come from another side to those who have striven to combat the erroneous view that Early Christian art was nothing more than classical art in decadence. The very features for which Hellenistic art was once praised are now condemned as its worst. . . . In no other field of research have archaeology and criticism better helped each other to overcome ungenerous tradition." If the echoes of the battle on this front, "*Orient oder Rom,*" are still to be heard, at any rate we no longer confuse the qualities of Hellenistic and Hellenic art; the deserved prestige of the latter no longer protects the former from destructive criticism.

In view of these facts, which it would be almost superflous to recapitulate, were it not for the peculiar attitude assumed by the author of the Greek theory and his followers, it should now be possible to discuss the subject calmly and to substitute argument for rhetoric. However this may be, I propose to outline here the evidences that exist to support the more obvious, but not therefore necessarily erroneous, theory of the Indian origin of the Buddha image in particular and of Indian iconography generally. Need I protect myself by saying that I do not mean by this to deny the existence of foreign elements and influences traceable in Indian art? I do mean, however, to imply that the proper time and place for their study and analysis is after, and not before, we have achieved a general understanding of the internal development of the art. The matter is of importance, not because the existence of foreign elements in any art (they exist in all arts) is not of great aesthetic significance, but just because when too much stress is laid upon this significance, the way to a clear apprehension of the general development of the art is obscured.[2] The subject has bulked already far too largely in the literature of Indian

1. To this, and numerous other remarks by M. Foucher in the same vein, sometimes more suggestive of propaganda than of sober science, I might well reply in the recent words of Dr. Salmony (*Die Rassenfrage in der Indienforschung*, in *Socialistischen Monatsheft*, *Heft* 8, 1926) "*Man darf ruhig sagen: Das europaische Urteil wurde bisher durch den Drang nach Selbstbehauptung verfälscht.*" In scientific writings, references to the nationality of those who do not or may not agree with us are not always in the best of taste; not all of M. Foucher's eloquence can make them gracious, and in any case they are no good substitute for reasoned argument.

As a matter of fact, Indian (and Japanese) scholars have shown a singular humility, and perhaps some timidity, in their ready acceptance of all the results of European scholarship; see, for example, Gauranganath Banerjee, *The Art of Gandhara*, and *Hellenism in Ancient India*. Most of those who have expressed doubts regarding the Foucher theory have been European (Havell, Cohn, Laufer, Goloubew, Sirén, Kramrisch, etc.).

2. As remarked by Laufer, *Das Citralakṣaṇa*, p. viii, note 1.

With some authors, Indo-Greek art has become a veritable obsession. The extent to which the dependence of Asiatic on Greek art has been pressed may be illustrated by the following examples: M. Blochet (*Gaz. des Beaux-Arts*, V, p. 114) recognizes Greek elements in Pahāṛī Rājput drawings, "*dans laquelle on retrouve toutes* [!] *les caractéristiques de l'art indo-grec du Gandhara,*" and remarks that in the twelfth and thirteenth centuries "*les temples brahmaniques sont des répliques du Mausolée qu'Artémise avait fait construire et decorer par des praticiens grecs.*" G. de Lorenzo (*India e Buddhismo Antico*, p. 45) suggests that Greek art, transformed and transported by Buddhism, may have animated the ancient art of the Aztecs and Incas of America. Jouveau-Dubreuil, *The Pallavas*, p. 7, calls the sculptures of Amaravātī "almost entirely Roman in workmanship."

art; my object in discussing it here is not so much to continue the controversy as to dismiss it.[3]

The subject can best be expounded under a series of heads, as follows: (1) What is the Buddha image? (2) The early representation of deities by means of symbols. (3) The necessity for a Buddha image. (4) Elements of the later anthropomorphic iconography already present in early Indian art. (5) Style and content: differentiation of Indian and Hellenistic types. (6) Dating of Gandhāra and Mathurā Buddhas.

1. WHAT IS THE BUDDHA IMAGE?

By the Buddha image, the ultimate origin of which is in question, I understand to be meant both the earliest Indian examples and the fully developed type as we meet with it in Gupta and mediaeval India, and in Farther India and the Far East. There can be no doubt that this fully developed type is the subject of M. Foucher's thesis, for he is careful to extend his filiation throughout the area and periods referred to. As he has also pointed out, the question of the origin of Jaina and Brahmanical types and iconography is equally involved; the Jaina figures, on account of their close resemblance to those of the Buddha, and because of the parallelism of the Jaina and Buddhist development, are here considered together with the Buddha type, while the Brahmanical figures, in order to avoid too great an extension of the field to be examined, are only incidentally referred to. The question of the origin of Bodhisattva types is inseparable from that of the origin of the Buddha figure.

It will suffice to illustrate a few examples of the fully developed type of which the beginnings are to be discussed. In plastic and ethnic character these figures are products of the age and place in which they are found, at the same time that their descent from some common ancestor is evident. Iconographically the types of Buddhas and even of Bodhisattvas (we are not here concerned with the later differentiation of innumerable many-armed forms) are few. For seated Buddhas there are five positions, one in which both hands held at the breast form the *dharmacakra mudrā*, one in which both hands rest palms upward on the lap in *dhyāna mudrā*, and three in which the left hand rests in the same way on the lap, the right hand either hanging over the right knee (*bhūmisparśa mudrā*) or resting on the knee palm upwards in *varada mudrā*, or raised in *abhaya mudrā*. Sometimes the left hand grasps the folds of the robe. In standing images the right hand is generally raised in *abhaya mudrā*, while the left holds the folds of the robe. Finally, there are reclining images. The robe in some cases covers one, in others both, shoulders. The drapery clings closely to the figure, and is felt to be almost transparent ("wet drapery"). The palms of the hands and soles of the feet are sometimes marked by symbols. Of physical peculiarities, the *uṣṇīṣa* or protuberance on the crown of the head is very evident, the *ūrṇā* or tuft of fine hair between the brows is commonly found, and the fingers are sometimes webbed. The hair is represented by short curls, turned to the right, and

3. I have quite recently (*The Indian Origin of the Buddha Image*, in *Journ. Am. Or. Soc.*, XLVI, 1926) assembled a series of quotations, mainly from authors committed to the Greek theory, sufficient to suggest the outlines of the true history of the Buddha image. That the reader will have consulted these references is here taken for granted. I may also refer to a review of the last published part of *L'art gréco-bouddhique du Gandhara*, published in the *Ostasiatische Zeitschrift*, N. F., 1, 1924, pp. 51-53, and to the essay on Buddhist primitives in my *Dance of Siva;* in the latter I would now present certain points in a different way.

forming little protuberances which cover the whole of the head and the *uṣṇīṣa*. The ears are elongated by the weight of earrings worn before the adoption of the monastic robes. Some kind of confusion between the Buddha and Bodhisattva type is indicated by the existence of a Buddha type with crown and jewels; strictly and normally, the Buddha should be represented in monastic robes, the Bodhisattva, whether Siddhārtha or any other, in secular royal costume. The Bodhisattvas are represented in less rigid positions, never, for example, with hands in *dhyāna mudrā;* they are commonly distinguished by attributes held in the right or left hand, Vajrapāṇi by the *vajra*, Padmapāṇi by the rose lotus, Avalokiteśvara by the blue lotus, Maitreya by the *amṛta* flask; these attributes may be held in either hand, but the right hand is often raised in the pose of exposition (*vyyākhyāna mudrā* or *cin mudrā*, sometimes called *vitarka*). Bodhisattvas are further distinguished by symbols indicated in the headdress, for example the Dhyāni Buddhas in the crowns of Avalokiteśvara and Mañjuśrī, the stupa in that of Maitreya; and in some cases by their "vehicles," Mañjusrī, for example, often riding on a lion. Each and all of these deities are almost invariably represented as seated or standing on an expanded rose lotus flower, with or without a lion throne or "vehicle" in addition. Jinas or Tīrthaṁkaras are represented like Buddhas seated in *dhyāna mudrā*, but generally nude, and otherwise only to be distinguished by special signs, such as the *śrīvatsa* symbol on Mahāvīra's breast, or by their attendants.

Fundamentally then, there are two Buddha-Jina types to be considered, that of the seated Buddha or Jina with hands resting in the lap or in one of a few other positions and that of the standing figure with the right hand raised in *abhaya mudrā*, both types being represented in monastic robes, and neither carrying attributes; and one Bodhisattva type, seated or standing, in secular costume and usually carrying attributes.

The fully evolved types described above are illustrated in Figs. 1, 5, 31, 40, 62-64, 66-73.

2. THE EARLY REPRESENTATION OF DEITIES BY MEANS OF SYMBOLS

It is extremely doubtful whether any of the Vedic deities were anthropomorphically represented in the Vedic period, that is to say, before the time of Buddha. References to images, however, become common in the later additions to the Brāhmaṇas and Sūtras and in the Epics; while a well-known passage of Patañjali, commenting on Pāṇini (V., 3, 99) refers to the exhibition of images of Śiva, Skanda, and Viśākha. Very probably, we may regard the symbolic method as, broadly speaking, Aryan, the anthropomorphic as aboriginal (Dravidian), or as respectively "Northern" and "Southern" in Strzygowski's sense. Images may have been characteristic of aboriginal religious cults from a remote time, only making their appearance in Brahmanical literature at the time when popular belief was actively affecting Brahmanical culture, that is to say in the early theistic period, when *pūjā* begins to replace *yajña*. We find traces of this aboriginal iconolatry not only in the early figures of Yakṣas, but also in such passages of the Gṛhya Sūtras as refer to the moving about of the images of bucolic deities, and the making of images of Nāgas for the Nāga Bali. In the early votive terra cottas, all apparently non-Buddhist, and usually representing goddesses, and as a subordinate element in early Buddhist and Jaina art, we find a well-developed and quite explicit popular iconography.

Here, however, we are concerned with the symbolic or aniconic method, which was at one time so universal, at least in orthodox and official circles, as to constitute by itself a

2—*Yakṣa (Pārkham)*
III Cent. B. C.

3—*Yakṣa (Patna)*
II Cent. B. C.

4—“*Bodhisattva*” (*Buddha*)
(*Sārnāth*) 123 *A. D.*

5—*Buddha (Mathurā)*
V Cent. A. D.

Stylistic Sequence of Yakṣa and Buddha Figures

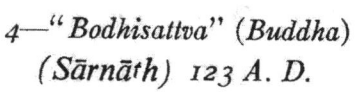

6—*Maues*

7—*Azes*

8—*Kadapha*

9—*Ujjain*

10—*Kaniṣka*

11—*Kaniṣka*

12—*Kaniṣka*

6–8, Supposed (by some) and 9-12, Actual Buddha Figures on Coins

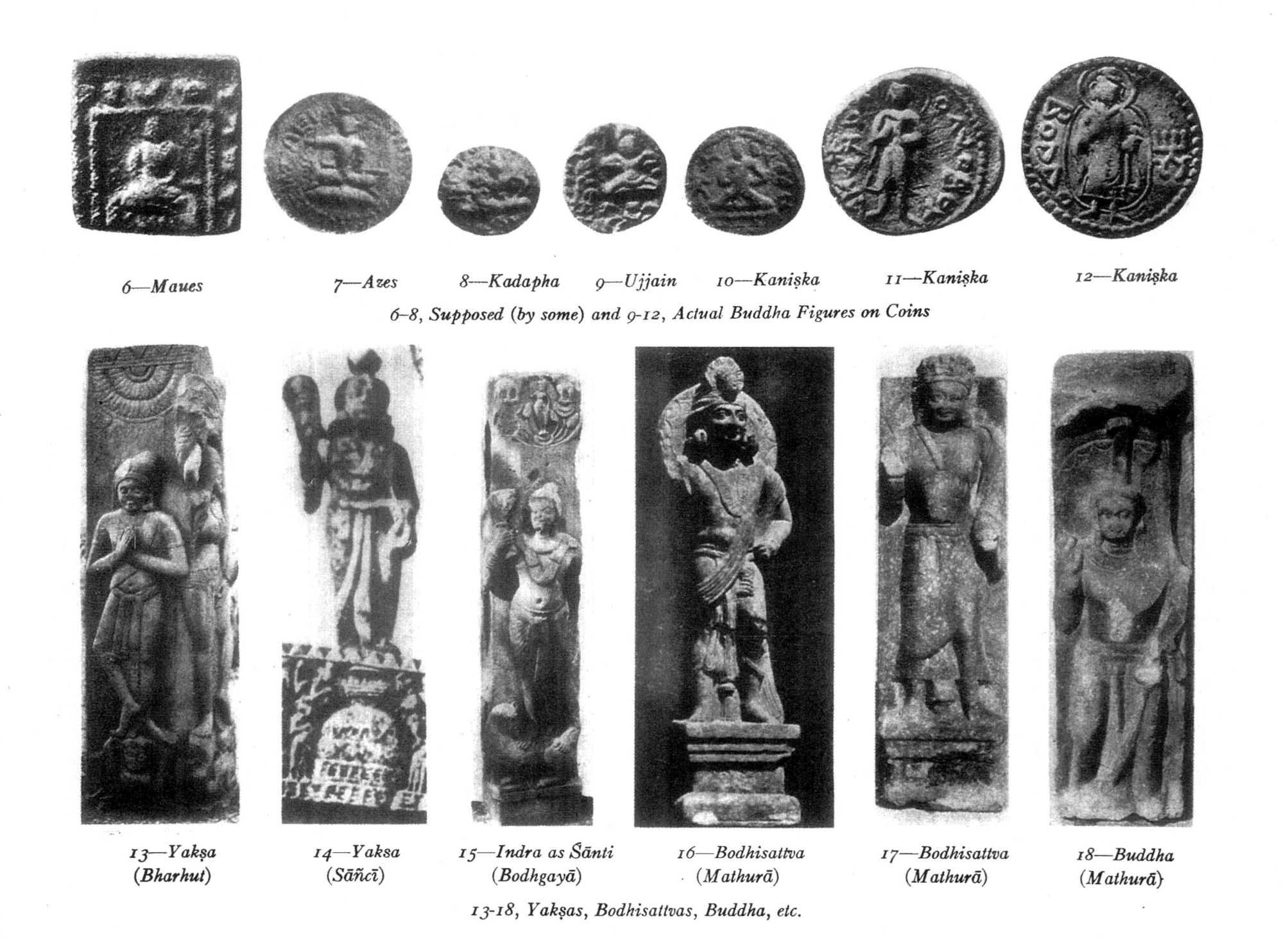

13—*Yakṣa* (*Bharhut*)

14—*Yaksa* (*Sāñcī*)

15—*Indra as Śānti* (*Bodhgayā*)

16—*Bodhisattva* (*Mathurā*)

17—*Bodhisattva* (*Mathurā*)

18—*Buddha* (*Mathurā*)

13-18, Yakṣas, Bodhisattvas, Buddha, etc.

complete artistic vocabulary and an iconography without icons. Of the symbols in use, those found on the punch-marked coins and early cast and struck coins include several hundred varieties; but some are much commoner than others.

Amongst these symbols, some of the commonest are the bull, *caitya-vṛkṣa* (railed sacred tree), mountain with one or several peaks (so-called *caitya* of numismatists), river, solar symbols (several varieties, all wheel-like), "*nandi-pada*" (circle surmounted by stemless trident), *triśūla* (trident part of the last without the circle), svastika, lotus, bow and arrow. I cannot here go into the evidence proving that neither the mountain nor the bow and arrow represent a stupa;[4] taking this for granted, it will be observed that none of these symbols, though most of them are used by Buddhists and Jainas in the early art, is in itself any more Buddhist or Jaina than it is Brahmanical, or simply Indian. The whole series constituted an assemblage of forms so explicit that, as the *Visuddhi Magga* informs us, an expert banker could tell from the marks at what place and mint the coin had been stamped. Each sign had a definite meaning, sometimes secular, sometimes sectarian.

M. Foucher has rightly observed that the beginnings of Buddhist art are characterized by the use of some of these symbols and one or two others; and that they were used to designate the presence of the Buddha in the story-telling reliefs of Bhārhut and Sāñcī, where no anthropomorphic representation of the Master can be found, that is to say, so far as the last incarnation is concerned. Thus in the long *Abhiniṣkramaṇa* scene (Fig. 19) Siddhārtha's presence on Kanthaka is indicated only by the royal umbrella borne beside

4. A much rarer symbol found on certain coins (e. g., Amoghabhūti, 100–150 B. C.) is commonly called a square stupa. Actually all that it represents is a railed umbrella (*chatra*) like those represented in relief at Gayā (Cunningham, *Mahābodhi*, pl. IX, fig. 14), and like the *harmikā* of the great stupa at Sārnāth, thus conceivably designating, though not representing, a stupa. A stupa would naturally be represented as a dome within and rising above a railing. Something of this kind is to be seen on certain Āndhra coins (Rapson, *Coins of the Andhra Dynasty*, pl. VIII, nos. 235, 236, etc.); but these suggest not the ordinary Buddhist stupa but the unusual type with a square railing and ovoid body seen in one relief at Amarāvatī (Fergusson, *Tree and Serpent Worship*, pl. LXXXVI) and one at Sāñcī, *ibid.*, pl. XXXII), both associated with bearded, apparently not Buddhist, ascetics. Regular stupas are first unmistakably represented on Gupta seals (Spooner, *Excavations at Basāṛh*, *A. S. I.*, *A. R.*, 1913–14, pl. XLVI, no. 159).

As regards the many-arched mountain, it may be remarked that this type is found on certain coins in unmistakably Hindu associations, e. g., on the coins of Svāmi Brahmaṇya Yaudheya, accompanying a six-headed Kārttikkeya, where a stupa would be meaningless. Apparently the interpretation of this type as a *caitya* (in the sense of stupa) has resulted from an *a priori* conviction that the coin symbols must be Buddhist, and secondly, from the necessity that was felt to find a prototype for the *parinirvāṇa* symbols of the reliefs. A comparative study of the abstract formulae used in Indian landscape compositions (e. g., the Maṇḍor stele, Govardhana-dhara composition, Bhandarkar, *Two Sculptures at Mandor*, *A. S. I.*, *A. R.*, 1905-06; or my *Rajput Painting*, pl. 2, or Petrucci's comment on this, *Burlington Maga ine*, V, 29, 1916), and likewise in early Western Asiatic and Eastern Mediterranean art would have indicated the true significance. It is quite probable that the "caitya" of three arches surmounted by a crescent represented Śiva, "the three-peaked mountain being originally the god" (Hopkins, *Epic Mythology*, p. 220). Śiva is said to have been the tutelary deity of the Śākyas (*Ep. Ind.*, V, p. 3).

One further point: the word *caitya* (Pali, *cetiya*) ought not to be used as though it were synonymous with stupa, nor as a purely Buddhist term. In the Epics, *caitya* usually means a *caitya-vṛkṣa*: in the (mediaeval) *Prabandhacintāmaṇi*, always a temple. In Buddhist literature the reference is sometimes to sacred trees, sometimes to stupas; two sacred trees with their altars represented at Bharhut are described in the contemporary inscriptions as *cetiyas* (Cunningham, *Bharhut*, Pls. XLIII, 4 and XLVIII, 6). The *Yakkha cetiya* so often mentioned in Buddhist and Jaina literature are in some cases *caityavṛksas* with an altar, in others, temples with images. Any holystead is a *caitya*, notwithstanding that the word is said to be derived from a root *ci*, to build or pile up; cannot the word, perhaps, be connected with *cit*, and understood to mean an object to be meditated upon?

The proper designation of the "nandipada", also often miscalled *vardhamāna*, is unknown. These and other coin symbols will be discussed at greater length in a forthcoming number of the *Ostasiatische Zeitschrift*.

him; his sojourn in the wilderness is indicated by foot-prints (*pāduka*); and the First Meditation by the central railed *caitya-vṛkṣa*. Some of these symbols taken alone came to be used to designate the Four Great Events (afterwards eight) of the Buddha's life: I am rather doubtful of the nativity symbols, but certainly the Bodhi-tree (a similar *caitya-vṛkṣa*) designated the Enlightenment, the *Dharma-cakra* (Wheel), the First Sermon, and the stupa, the Parinirvāṇa. Further detail is immaterial for present purposes. It need only be remarked that M. Foucher assumes that the symbols were thus used by Buddhists in the first place upon *signacula*, little documents carried away by pilgrims visiting the sacred sites of the Four Great Events.[5] Presumably these would have been of terra cotta or metal; but no trace of such objects has ever been found, and such early terra cottas as are known in some abundance are, as indicated above, of a quite different sort. The point, however, is unnecessary to M. Foucher's argument, as in any case an abundance of symbols was available to be made use of by every sect according to its own needs; and that each actually did so is only another illustration of the general rule that styles of art, in India, are not sectarian. M. Foucher's statement of the theory is only misleading to the extent that he implies that there was anything especially Buddhist about the process. When however he goes on to say[6] that the sculptors of Bhārhut, Bodhgayā, and Sāñcī "*devaient se sentir terriblement gênés par cette incapacité ou cette interdiction d'introduire dans leurs compositions les plus compliquées l'image du héros principal*" he is only preparing the way for the later revelation from Gandhāra; as he has admitted elsewhere, there existed neither an incapacity (the same sculptors represented the Buddha freely as a human being in previous incarnations) nor an interdiction (for nothing of the kind can be found in Buddhist literature), and, as is readily apparent, the sculptor was by no means embarrassed, but in fact perfectly successful in telling his story.[7] It is hardly to be supposed that the meaning of these reliefs needed to be explained to contemporary Buddhists.

At this point an earlier than Gandhāra indebtedness of Indian art to that of Greece has been inferred in more than one connection. Della Setta, endorsed by Foucher, has pointed

5. *Beginnings of Buddhist Art*, p. 11.

6. *L'art gréco-bouddhique du Gandhara*, I, p. 612.

7. It may as well be observed here that the later representation of the Buddha figure in Indian art is not the same thing as the introduction of a naturalistic *style;* a new object, the human figure, is introduced where it had been absent, but this figure is treated in the traditional abstract manner. The only naturalistic *style* in question is that of Gandhāra. No phase of Indian art can be described as naturalistic in this sense; if we sometimes call the early style realistic, this only means that its theme is corporeal rather than spiritual.

The tendency to represent the human figure need not involve a naturalistic style: in Greek art the use of the figure and a naturalistic style are associated; in Indian art it is not the appearance, but the significance of objects, human or otherwise, that is sought for. In Greek art the emphasis is laid upon the object; in an abstract art it is not the object, but a concept that stands before us.

Every work of art is of course to some extent a compromise between the two points of view, naturalistic and abstract (or expressionistic); but what it is important to observe here is that the two extremes are contrasted, not in Indian Buddhist art before and after the introduction of the cult image (the Indian style remaining abstract throughout, whether it represents a sacred tree or a Buddha figure), but in Indian and Hellenistic art, respectively abstract and naturalistic. We are not here discussing questions of merit; as remarked by H. Frankfort in a clear definition of terms (*Studies in Early Pottery of the Near East*, I, London, 1924, p. 18): "The sense of beauty or aesthetic activity may equally well find expression in both ways." The only possibility of embarrassment is found when the artist for arbitrary reasons adopts one of these styles opposed to his innate idiosyncracy; Asiatic art under European influence in the nineteenth century affords many examples of such embarrassment. It is ridiculous to speak of embarrassment at Sāñcī, or to suppose that a decadent naturalistic art could have inspired a young and vigorous abstract art.

19—Abhiniṣkramaṇa (Great Renunciation) (Sāñcī)

20—Buddha Triad (Sāñcī)

21—First Sermon (Mathurā)

22—Bowl Relic and Great Enlightenment (Mathurā)

23—Sujātā's Offering (Sāñcī)

Aniconic Representations of the Buddha. Sāñcī and Mathurā

24—*Nāga* (*Pāṭaliputra*)

25—*Seated Figures* (*Bharhut*)

26—*Nāga Erāpata Worshipping Buddha* (*Bharhut*)

27—*Teacher and Disciples* (*Bharhut*)

28—*The Parinirvāṇa* (*Bharhut*)

29—*Vessantara Jātaka* (*Bharhut*)

Aniconic Representations of Buddha; Early Nāga, Bodhisattva, etc.

out that the representation of three-quarters profile, and the use of continuous narration are illustrated somewhat earlier in Greece than in India. Strzygowski holds that the method of continuous narration was developed in the Hellenistic Near East. Marshall believes Western influences felt through Bactria may account for the artistic progress recognizable at Sāñcī; but, as recently observed by Rostovtzeff, "we know so little of Bactrian art that it is a mistake in method to explain '*ignotum per ignotius*'." It has not yet been suggested that inverted perspective and vertical projection are of Hellenistic origin (see Dalton, *East Christian Art*, p. 166). But a discussion of these points lies outside the scope of the present essay, as in any case these technical methods antedate Gandhāra.

Nor need anything further be said upon the subject of the symbolic language, except to remark that it remained in use, particularly at Amarāvatī, but also in Mathurā, for some time subsequent to the introduction of the anthropomorphic image.

For aniconic representations of Buddha referred to in this section see Figs. 19-23, 26, 28.

3. THE NECESSITY FOR A BUDDHA IMAGE

Inasmuch as neither the Upaniṣads nor Buddhism nor Jainism, considered in their original character as systems of thought, contemplated the worship (*pūjā*) of any personal deity, it may well be asked how it came to pass that Hinduism, Buddhism, and Jainism alike became "idolatrous" religions. The answer to this question was admirably expressed by Jacobi over forty years ago:[8] "I believe that this worship had nothing to do with original Buddhism or Jainism, that it did not originate with the monks, but with the lay community, when the people in general felt the want of a higher cult than that of their rude deities and demons, when the religious development of India found in Bhakti the supreme means of salvation. Therefore instead of seeing in the Buddhists the originals and in the Jainas the imitators, with regard to the erection of temples and worship of statues, we assume that both sects were, independently of each other, brought to adopt this practice by the perpetual and irresistible influence of the religious development of the people in India."

Bhakti, as is well known, means loving devotion, loyalty, attachment, service to one who is *Bhagavata*, worshipful, adorable, Lord, and he who feels such devotion and is devoted to any such being, is called *Bhāgavata* or *Bhaktā*. The conception comes into prominence together with, and is inseparably bound up with, the development of theistic cults in India, as these are with the making of images and the building of temples. Theistic elements are recognizable in the Upaniṣads; the development, as proved by the inscription of Heliodora, who calls himself a Bhāgavata, with reference to Viṣṇu, was already advanced in the second century B. C. Vaiṣṇava inscriptions, indeed, of the third or fourth century B. C. have been found at Nagarī (Madhyamikā) near Chitor. The most famous Bhakti scripture is the *Bhagavad Gītā* referred to above, a work that must have been composed before the beginning of the Christian era, and perhaps about the fourth century B. C. "Be assured, O son of Kunti," says Kṛṣṇa, "that none who is devoted to Me is lost." In the same way the Buddhist *Majjhima Nikāya* assures us that even those who have not yet entered the Paths "are sure of heaven if they have love and faith toward Me."

8. Jacobi, *Gaina Sūtras*, in *S. B. E.*, XXII, 1884, p. xxi.

Much discussion has been devoted to the question of the origin of Bhakti cults. Let us examine the usage of the word. Outside the field of religion revealed in Vedic literature there lay a world of popular beliefs including the worship of Yakṣas and Nāgas as tutelary divinities or *genii loci*, and of feminine divinities, powers of fertility.[9] Buddhist and Jaina texts contain many references to the cult or shrines of Yakṣas or Nāgas.[10] To what extent the *Yakkha-cetiya* (*Yakṣa caityas*) of Buddhist texts may have been actual temples, or merely "haunts" (*bhavana*) marked by the establishment of a throne, or rather altar, beneath a sacred tree or beside a lake need not concern us here. What does concern us here is the importance of these divinities, and the relation that existed between them and their worshippers. There is no reason to doubt the tradition preserved in the Tibetan *Dulva* that the Śākyas were accustomed to present all newborn children before the image of the Yakṣa Śākya-vardhana, evidently the tutelary deity of the clan.[11] Another Tibetan source relates that a gatekeeper of Vaiśāli, in the Buddha's lifetime, was reborn among the spirits, and requested the inhabitants of Vaiśāli to confer on him the status of a Yakṣa, in return for which he would warn them of any danger threatening them, "So they caused a Yakṣa statue to be prepared and hung a bell round its neck. Then they set it up in the gatehouse, and provided it with oblations and garlands along with dance and song to the sound of musical instruments."[12] In the *Mahābhārata*, a Yakṣiṇī is referred to as receiving a daily service and cult at Rājagṛha, and another Yakṣiṇī shrine was "world-renowned." The city of Nandivardhana in Magadha seems to have been called after the tutelary Yakṣas Nandi and Vardha.[13] Jaina and Buddhist traditions are in agreement as to the names of some of the Yakṣa *caityas*. The *Mahāvaṁsa*, Chapter X, describes the cult of Yakṣas in Ceylon. Yakṣas are usually gentle; sometimes they act as familiars or guardian angels of individuals.[14]

The Yakṣa Kuvera (Vaiśravaṇa, Vaiśramaṇa), who is closely associated with Śiva, and Regent of the North, thus one of the Four Great Kings, the Lokapālas, is a very powerful genius. But the term "Yakṣa" seems once to have implied something more than Kuvera or one of his attendants. *Yakṣattva* in the *Rāmāyaṇa* is spoken of as a valued boon; like immortality, it is bestowed by the gods when rightly propitiated.[15] This older and wider significance, as remarked by Kern,[16] is sometimes met with in Buddhist references to

9. Both Yakṣas and Nāgas are aboriginal, non-Aryan types. Macdonell's surmise (*Vedic Mythology*, p. 153) that the Aryans "doubtless found the cult (of Nāgas) extensively diffused among the natives when they spread over India, the land of serpents," has been curiously justified by the discovery of Nāga types on Indo-Sumerian seals (*A. S. I.*, *A. R.*, 1924-5, p. 61). See also Vogel, *Indian Serpent Lore*, and my article on Yakṣas to appear as a Smithsonian publication in 1928.

10. *Yakkha-Saṁyutta* of the *Saṁyutta Nikāya*, X, 4, Other references in Chanda, *Four Ancient Yakṣa Statues*. in *University of Calcutta, Journ. Dep. Letters*, IV, 1921 (pp. 5, 34-36 of the reprint).

11. Rockhill, *Life of the Buddha*, p. 17. The episode is twice represented at Amarāvatī (Fergusson, *Tree and Serpent Worship*, pls. LXIX and XCI, 4).

12. Schiefner, *Tibetan Tales from the Kah-gyur*, trans. Ralston, p. 81.

13. O. C. Gangoly, in *Modern Review*, Oct., 1919; and Chanda, *op. cit.*, with reference to a statement in the *Mahāmayurī*.

14. Hopkins, *Epic mythology*, p. 57; Foucher, *L'art gréco-bouddhique du Gandhara*, II, p. 40 ff. It is precisely the rôle of guardian angel that some Yakṣas play in relation to Buddhas and Jinas, in relation to Buddha, particularly the Yakṣa Vajrapāṇi.

15. *Rāmāyaṇa*, III, 11, 94; Hopkins, *op. cit.*, p. 67.

16. *Manual of Indian Buddhism*, p. 59. Foucher, *op. cit.*, insists on the cruel nature of Yakṣas as referred to in Buddhist texts; but this is usually where some story of miraculous conversion is related, and may well be designed to emphasize the marvel. That *ugra* Yakṣa types also existed need not be denied; but the familiar example of Kālī or of Śiva himself would show how little this need have interfered with their existence as objects of a Bhakti cult.

The subject of Yakṣas will be treated at some length in a Smithsonian publication in 1928. See also the admirable summary under *Yakkha* in Rhys Davids and Stede, *Pali Dictionary*.

Yaksas; Indra, for example, may be called a Yakṣa, and even the Buddha is glorified by Upāla in the *Majjhima Nikāya* as an *āhuneyyo yakkho utamapuggalo atulo.*

Many references to Nāga cults are scattered through the Buddhist texts. The Chinese pilgrims constantly refer to monasteries and stupas occupying sites originally haunted by Nāgas. Hsüan Tsang informs us that Nālandā was originally the name of a Nāga "and the monastery built by the side of a pool is therefore called after his name."[17]

The significance for us of these cults so widely diffused and so popular in ancient India will be apparent when, in the first place, we observe that the nature of the worship offered was in many respects similar to that offered in a Buddhist temple, including particularly the erection of statues and the offering of flowers, garlands, incense, and music; in the second place that Buddhism, like other religions in similar circumstances, constantly inherited the prestige of sites already sacred, as at Bodhgayā and Nālandā; and finally, and most important, that the designation *Bhagavata* is applied not alone to Vāsudeva (Viṣṇu),[18] to Śiva[19] and to Buddha,[20] but also to the Four Great Kings, the Mahārājas, Regents of the Quarters,[21] of whom some are Yakṣas and some Nāgas, and also to various Yakṣas and Nāgas specifically.[22]

Buddhism exhibited no hostility to these popular cults: the Buddha indeed expressly exhorts the Licchavi-Vajjis to continue "to honour and esteem and revere and support the Vajjian cetiyas in the city or outside it, and allow not proper offerings and rites as formerly given and performed to fall into desuetude," and so long as this were done, "so long may the Licchavi-Vajjis be expected not to decline but to prosper."[23]

Historically, the Bhāgavata cults of Yakṣas and Nāgas must have yielded only gradually and peacefully to the Bhāgavata cults of Viṣṇu and Buddha; the cult of Nāgas and Yakṣas, indeed, is still widely prevalent, and though I do not know that the term Bhagavata is still employed, the lower classes throughout India still worship innumerable local godlings of this character, and it is significant that the priesthood of the temples of such godlings is always non-Brāhman.[24] Officially, these cults were replaced by the "higher"

17. Beal, *Life of Hiuen Tsang*, p. 110; *Buddhist Records of the Western World*, pp. 63ff., 123, 149ff., 200.

18. Pāṇini, IV, 3, 98; inscription of Heliodora at Besnagar, proclaiming himself a Bhāgavata (D. R. Bhandarkar, *Excavations at Besnagar*, in *A. S. I., A. R.*, 1913-14 and 1914-15; R. G. Bhandarkar, *Vaiṣṇavism, Śaivism, and Minor Religious Systems*, p. 5; R. P. Chanda, *Archæology and Vaishnava Tradition*, in *Mem. A. S. I.*, 1920).

19. Patañjali mentions Śiva bhāgavatas (*in re* Pāṇini, V, 2, 76): Śiva is called Bhagavat in the *Atharvaśiras Upaniṣad*. Cf. *Mahābhārata*, XII, 18, 65: "Even after committing all crimes, men by mental worship of Śiva are freed from all sin" with *Bhagavad Gītā*, ix, 30.

20. E. g., *Bhagavato Saka Munino* at Bhārhut, also the Piprahwā vase inscription.

21. Pāṇini, IV, 3, 97, speaks of Bhakti directed to Mahārājas (not in a political sense as interpreted by Jayaswal, but with reference to the Four Great Kings, see Bhusari in *Ann. Bhandarkar Inst.*, VIII, 1926, p. 199); also in *Mahābhārata*, VIII, 45, 31, but here the Regent of the North is Soma (Hopkins, *Vedic Mythology*, p. 149).

22. Kubera, in *Mahābhārata*, V, 192, 42 ff. (Hopkins, *Epic Mythology*, p. 145); Māṇibhadra, image and inscription from Pawāyā where his worshippers, the *goṣṭha* or corporation (guild) who installed the image, describe themselves as Māṇibhadra-bhaktā (M. B. Garde, *The Site of Padumāvatī*, in *A. S. I., A. R.*, 1914-15, pt. I; Chanda, *op. cit.*); the Nāga Dadhikarṇa, Mathurā inscription, Lüders list, no. 85; Nāgas in the Mathurā Museum, Vogel, *Catalogue*, Nos. C 13 and C 21.

23. *Anguttara Nikāya.* It need hardly be pointed out again that *caitya, cetiya,* signifies any kind of holystead such as a sacred tree, grove, or temple, not necessarily a stupa.

24. For these cults at the present day see Hutchinson and Vogel, *History of Basohli State*, in *Journ. Panjab Hist. Soc.*, IV, 2, 1916, p. 118; S. C. Mitra, *On the Worship of the Pipal Tree in North Bihar*, in *J. B. O. R. S.*, VI, 1920, p. 572, and *The Village Deities of North Bengal*, in *Hindustan Review*, Feb., 1922; Callaway, *Yakkun Nattanawā . . . Ceylon System of Demonology . . .*, London, 1829; R. B. Whitehead, *The Village Gods of Southern India*, London and Calcutta, 1916; Fergusson, *Tree and Serpent Worship*, p. 258; Longhurst, *Tree and Serpent Worship in Southern India*, in *A. S. I., A. R., Southern Circle*, 1914-15; R. E. Enthoven, *Bombay Folklore*, 1924; E. Upham, *History and Doctrine of Buddhism*, 1829.

faiths, Vaiṣṇava, Saiva, Bauddha, and Jaina; but even officially the Nāgas and Yakṣas were not dismissed, as the gods of ancient Ireland were dismissed by the Christian monks, but represented as worshippers or guardians of the Buddha or Jina. Nor could the "higher religions," when from systems of pure thought and of monastic discipline they developed into popular faiths, have succeeded in securing the adhesion of the mass of the people had they not both tolerated and reflected popular beliefs. Iconolatry, ritual,[25] devotion, profound preoccupations of the popular Indian non-Aryan consciousness, made of Buddhism, Jainism, and Hinduism what they are, and that is something other than they were in their intellectual inception. The sculptures themselves (Figs. 26, 28) bear witness to the power of the spirit of devotion.

If we are to believe the *Nidānakathā*, Sujātā mistook the Bodhisattva for the sylvan deity for whom her offering of milk-rice had been originally intended (Fig. 23); the story proves at least that Buddhists conceived that such a mistake might very naturally have been made. Later on, to simple folk, statues of Yakṣas and Buddhas, both associated with trees, both legitimately spoken of as Bhagavata, "The Lord," both worshipped with flowers, garlands, and incense, must have looked very much alike.[26] Nor can we altogether ignore the fact that figures of a Buddha or Jina protected by a many-headed Nāga, whose hoods form a canopy above their heads, bear, no less than certain Vaiṣṇava types (Balarāma, and Viṣṇu Anantaśayana), a striking resemblance to an actual Nāga, as represented in the early sculptures—having a human body, but with serpent hoods rising from a point on the back behind the shoulders. We shall presently recognize a sculptural type which represents equally well a *padmapāṇi* Yakṣa and a Bodhisattva Padmapāṇi.

We have traced above, in popular Indian religion, sources of theism, image worship, and devotion, as we find them appearing in orthodox Brāhmanism and Buddhism toward the beginning of the Christian era, in Buddhism as tendencies that point toward the Mahāyāna. When we realize in this way how naturally the demand for a Buddha image must have arisen, and how readily available were suitable types,[27] we may be less inclined to jump to the conclusion that the cult image of the Tathāgata was of extra-Indian origin. That such had really been the case we could only believe, against all *a priori* probabilities, if in fact the earliest Indian Buddha figures, instead of perpetuating the plastic tradition and repeating the iconographic formulae of the old Indian school, had really resembled Hellenistic prototypes. Even the most ardent advocates of the Greek theory cannot claim so

25. It is interesting to recall in passing the close parallels that exist between Buddhist (and Hindu) and Christian ritual, such as the use of lights, incense, bells, rosaries, tonsure, formal gestures, and music. These cult elements probably found their way into the Christian office through Alexandria and Coptic monasticism during the first few centuries of the Christian era (cf. Garbe, *Indien und Christentum;* and H. Berstl, *Indo-koptische Kunst*, pp. 180, 188, in *Jahrb. as. Kunst*, 1924). Thus the pagan elements surviving in Christian practice may be traced back to a remote pre-Buddhist and non-Aryan Indian antiquity; and the problems here discussed are found to possess an interest not exclusively Indian, but bound up with the general history of religion and art. On *bhakti* and *pūjā* see de La Vallée Poussin, *Indo-Européens et Indo-Iraniens: l'Inde jusque vers 300 av. J. C.*, 1924, pp. 314 ff., and Charpentier, *Über den Begriff und die Etymologie von pūjā* in *Festgabe Hermann Jacobi*, 1926.

26. Apparently one of the *caityas* of Vaiśālī was a banyan tree which was the abode of a Yakṣa by name Gotama. Remembering that in early Buddhism the Bodhi-tree is generally spoken of as a banyan (though always represented in art as *Ficus religiosa*) it will be seen that in this particular case a transference of significance from a Bhagavata Yakṣa Gotama to the Bhagavata Gautama Śākya-muni would have been especially easy. See Chanda, *Mediaeval Sculpture in Eastern India*, in *Calcutta Univ. Journal, Dept. Letters*, III, 1920, pp. 232 f.

27. See the next section.

much as this; nor would it be possible to put forward such a claim with Friar Bala's Bodhisattva and the Kaṭrā and Aṇyor Mathurā Buddhas before our eyes.

4. ELEMENTS OF THE LATER ANTHROPOMORPHIC ICONOGRAPHY ALREADY PRESENT IN EARLY INDIAN ART

Actual remains and literary evidences abundantly prove that images of divinities and of human beings, both in relief and in the round, existed already in the third and second centuries B. C., and it is very possible that similar figures in precious metal or impermanent materials had been made at a still earlier date. Even in specifically Buddhist art we find the Bodhisattva freely represented in human form in Jātaka illustrations, side by side with the purely symbolic indications of Gautama as Bodhisattva (Siddhārtha) or as Buddha (Tathāgata).[28] Craftsmen capable of producing the Pārkham and Patna images, and the reliefs at Bhārhut and Sāñcī would have had no difficulty in representing Gautama in human form had they been required to do so.

India had long associated the attainment of higher stations of consciousness and the perception of ultimate truths with the practice of disciplined meditation, and had long been familiar with ascetic teachers. When a Buddha image was required, he would naturally be represented either as an adept or as a teacher; conceptions that immediately connote, in the one case the cross-legged seance,[29] hands at rest in the lap, and abstracted gaze directed toward the tip of the nose, in the other, the same seance, but with the right hand raised, the left resting on the hip, and a more active demeanor. The practice of yoga is older, of course, than Buddhism or Jainism and neither of these religions did more than adopt and adapt the existing technique of contemplation. A beautiful description of the seated yogī will be found in the *Bhagavad Gītā*, VI, 10-21; condensed as follows:

"Abiding alone in a secret place, without craving and without possessions, with thought and self controlled, he shall take his seat upon a firm seat, neither over-high nor over-low making the mind single-pointed, with the working of the intellect and senses held in check, with body, head and neck maintained in perfect equipoise, looking not round about him, so let him meditate, and thereby reach the peace of the Uttermost Abyss; and the likeness of one such, who knows the boundless joy that lies beyond the senses and is grasped by intuition, and who is free from longing for all desirable things, is that of a lamp in a windless place, that does not flicker."

A briefer description will be found in the canonical Buddhist *Dīgha Nikāya*, sutta 22:

"And how, O monks, does a monk live, observant of the body?

"Whereas, O monks, a monk, retiring to the forest, or to the foot of a tree, or to some other uninhabited spot, sits him down cross-legged, with body erect and contemplative faculty intent . . . training himself to be conscious of all his expirations and inspirations."

28. The figure of the Bodhisattva, Siddhārtha, is *not* represented in certain reliefs which have been regarded as illustrating the Approach to the Bodhi-tree, at Bodhgayā and Sāñcī (Cunningham, *Mahābodhi*, pl. VIII, fig. 4, as interpreted by Bloch, *Notes on Bodh-Gayā*, in *A. S. I.*, *A. R.*, 1908-09; Maisey, *Sanchi*, pl. XVI; and Fergusson, *Tree and Serpent Worship*, pl. XXXIII).

29. Cf. *Bhagavad Gītā*, VI, 10-21, describing the firm and easy (*sthira-sukha*) seance of the yogi. I use the word *seance* to translate *āsana* in the sense of a mode of sitting, as I use *stance* to translate *sthānam*.

No new effort on the part of the sculptor was needed for the realization of these types, which appear already at Bhārhut, once in a relief of uncertain significance (Fig. 25) and once in a composition representing Digha instructing his disciples (Fig. 27).[30] Seated figures which have in fact been identified as Buddha are also found on coins of Maues (c. 100 B. C.) and Kadapha (Kadphises I, c. 40-78 A. D.).[31] In both coins we find the cross-legged seance. In the case of the Maues coin (Fig. 6) the two hands are folded in the lap; but there is a horizontal bar extended to the right which may be a sword or scepter, or possibly the back edge of a throne or seat. In the case of the Kadapha coins (Fig. 8), of which there are two closely related varieties, the right hand is raised, holding some hammer-like object, perhaps a scepter, the left hand rests on the thigh, and the elbow is extended, while the breadth of the shoulders and slenderness of the waist are conspicuous. It seems to me that these personages represent a king, and not a Buddha. The Kadapha type, however, apart from the object held in the hand, is exactly that of the early Mathurā Buddhas (Figs. 34-39) and of figures of kings or perhaps Bodhisattvas, and of Buddha, at Amarāvatī. The characteristic and vigorous gesture of the palm or clenched fist resting on the thigh is rarely met with in later art, but survives, for example, in certain mediaeval Bodhisattva types (Fig. 65) and is often used by Javanese actors at the present day.

More convincing than any of the types above referred to are the seated figures found on early Ujjain coins. One of these (Fig. 9) can hardly be anything but a Buddha, as it represents, to quote Cunningham's words, a "figure squatting in the native fashion beside a holy tree surrounded by a railing," and, moreover, squatting on a lotus seat. This is perhaps the earliest male figure so represented as seated upon an expanded lotus. However we cannot exactly date these coins; they can hardly be earlier than the first century A. D.[32] The type, however, is precisely that which appears on Kaniṣka's seated Buddha coins (Fig. 10), with the identifying designation.

As regards the physical peculiarities of the Buddha type, we find the *uṣṇīṣa* represented in the Indian fashion as a rounded cranial protuberance already in the case of the relief representing Indra as Śānti on one of the Bodhgayā railing pillars, dateable about 100 B. C.[33] Buddha-like heads with an *uṣṇīṣa*-like protuberance, and many short curls, are

30. Also in the unpublished relief from Bharhut, a scene from the *Vessantara Jātaka*, in which the Brahman Jujaka is seen seated cross-legged in his leaf hut. Berstl, *Indo-koptische Kunst*, in *Jahrb. as. Kunst*, I, 1924, has traced the westward migration of the "yogi-*motif*" about and somewhat before the beginning of the Christian era. He inferred its early occurrence in Indian sculpture but does not seem to have known the Bharhut examples above referred to. As a matter of fact, the *motif* has since been found on Indo-Sumerian seals probably to be dated well before 2000 B. C. (*A. S. I.*, *A. R.*, 1924-5, p. 61).

31. Maues: Longworth Dames, in *J. R. A. S.*, 1914, p. 793, calls it Buddha; Whitehead, *Cat. Coins in the Panjab Museum, Lahore*, p. 102 and pl. X, 31, calls it a king; Vincent Smith, *Cat. Coins in the Indian Museum, Calcutta*, p. 40 and pl. VIII, 4, calls it a deity or king; Gardner, *Cat. Coins in the British Museum, Greek and Scythian Kings of Bactria and India*, p. 71 and pl. XVII, 5, calls it a king with a sword on his knees. The similar but better preserved type on a coin of Azes, Gardner, *op. cit.*, pl. XVII, and *A. S. I.*, *A. R.*, 1912-13, pl. XL, 18, shows that the latter description should be correct.

Kadapha: Whitehead, *op. cit.*, pp. 181, 182 and references there cited; Marshall, *Excavations at Taxila*, in *A. S. I.*, *A. R.*, 1913-14, p. 44 and pl. XL, 53, 1914-15, p. 33 and pl. XXIX, 38, and 1915-16, p. 34 and pl. XXV, 18, 19. Both call it a seated Buddha, but cf. the coin of Huviṣka, seated king, crossed legs, with attributes in both hands, Vincent Smith, *Numismatic Notes, I*, in *J. B. A. S.*, 1897, fig. iv, also the Gandhāra sculpture in *A. S. I.*, *A. R.*, 1914-15, pl. X, 18.

32. Cunningham, *Coins of Ancient India*, p. 97 and pl. X, 7, 8, 10.

33. L. Bachofer, *Ein Pfeiler-Figur aus Bodh-Gaya*, *Jahrb. as. Kunst*, II, 1925; Sir J. H. Marshall, *J. R. A. S.*, 1908, p. 1096 and pl. IV. Stella Kramrisch describes this figure as psychologically a Buddha prototype (*Grundzüge der indischen Kunst*, p. 83). In general appearance it is nearer to the standing Bodhisattva types.

represented on several of the Bodhgayā railing medallions. There is, indeed, a prominence very suggestive of an *uṣṇīṣa* to be seen on the head of the Nāga figure on the Pāṭaliputra railing (Fig. 24). I cannot recall any pre-Kuṣāna sculpture in which an *ūrṇā* is represented, nor any earlier example of even a Buddha with webbed fingers than the Māṅkuwāṛ image (448/9 A. D., Fig. 61). In the representation of the hair in many curls, which does not appear until after the middle of the second century A. D., it is evident that literary tradition has been followed. It has been suggested, and is quite possible, that the webbed fingers represent what was at first a technical device, intended to avoid breakage.

Turning now to the standing figure in early Indian art, we find its chief iconographic peculiarities are the symmetrical stance, with well-separated feet, the raising of the right hand usually in the *abhaya* position,[34] and the placing of the left hand upon the thigh either clenched, or holding the folds of the robe. Later the left hand is generally somewhat raised, but still grasps the drapery. Unfortunately, the arms of the oldest Indian figures, the Pārkham (Fig. 2) and Patna (Fig. 3) Yakṣas[35] are missing. But the characteristic attitude of the early standing Buddhas is well seen in the case of a panel relief on one of the railing crossbars found by Waddell[36] at Pāṭaliputra (Fig. 24), representing a Nāga beside a tree; see also Fig. 47. In later, that is to say pre-Kuṣāna and early Kuṣāna sculpture the pose is so usual that we may fairly regard it as typical; Yakṣas, Nāgas, and goddesses are alike represented in this way. Sometimes the left hand rests simply on the hip (*kaṭyavalambita hasta*), sometimes it seems to grasp the drapery, sometimes, particularly in the case of the Bacchanalian Yakṣa and Nāga types (Fig. 49), it holds a flask suggesting the *amṛta* flask of Maitreya.

34. Regarding this *mudrā*, or *hasta*, which is the only one except the *añjali* common in early Indian art, it should be observed (1) that the hand is sometimes *vyāvṛtta*, sometimes *parivṛtta*, the latter position being usual in the later art, and (2) this hand serves apparently to indicate several meanings which are later more carefully differentiated. The various meanings of the *patāka* hand in dancing include removing fear, graciousness, benediction, taking an oath, addressing an audience, closing a dispute, and any of these are appropriate to the early usage; other meanings, such as "wave" require a *movement* of the hand (cf. *Mirror of Gesture*, p. 27). The treatment of gesture in Bharata's *Nāṭya Śāstra*, which may date back to the second century B. C., implies a long established tradition; for gesture language (which is one of the sixty-four *kalās*, accomplishments) in everyday life, see *Jātaka*, No. 546 (Cowell's translation, p. 182), where the "hands" employed seem to have been *śikhara* and *patāka*.

As regards the clenched fist (*muṣṭi*) of Mathurā types, I have not observed this in earlier Indian, or in Gandhāra types; the most suitable meaning given in *abhinaya* books is that of "steadiness." The energy of the gesture is enhanced by the holding of the elbows away from the waist; the arm thus held akimbo is characteristic of early Indian types, is found sparingly in mediaeval works (Fig. 65), and survives in the Javanese theater, while it is not seen in Gandhāra.

35. The equally ancient archaic Yakṣa at Deoriyā, Allahābād (Fig. 47) has the left hand on the hip; and this was almost certainly the same in the case of the Besnagar figure (Fig. 2).

For present purposes it is unnecessary to enter upon the controversy as to whether these figures represent pre-Mauryan kings, or represent Yakṣas, of Maurya and Śuṅga date. I now agree with Chanda (*Four Ancient Yakṣa Statues*, Calcutta, 1921) and others in taking the latter view. It is not disputed that these are the oldest known examples of Indian stone sculpture in the round (recent Indo-Sumerian discoveries aside), and represent the true "primitives" of an original and indigenous style.

36. L. A. Waddell, *Report on the Excavations at Pataliputra*, Calcutta, 1903, pl. 1. Other early examples are found on coins, e. g., Dhara Ghoṣa, Audumbara, Cunningham, *Coins of Ancient India*, pl. IV, 1; early Taxila, *ibid.*, pl. II, 14; early Kosāmbi, *ibid.*, pl. V, 15. Credit is due to Waddell, who, although a subscriber to the Greek theory and ardent admirer of Gandhāra art, remarked that "Buddhism . . . manifestly took the preëxisting images of the Brahmanist gods such as we see on the Bhārhut stupa as their models" (*Evolution of the Buddhist Cult, its Gods, Images and Art*, in *Imp. and As. Qtly. Review*, Jan., 1912); and equally to Laufer (*Das Citralakṣaṇa*, p. 18): "*Wenn die Buddhisten das ganze brahmanische Göttersystem adoptiert haben, dann ist auch die grosste Wahrscheinlichkeit vorhanden, dass sie die Ikonographie dieser empfangen haben; es ist undenkbar, dass sie die kunstlerische Gestaltung selbst erfunden haben sollten.*"

The phylogeny of the standing Bodhisattva types is even clearer, because here the secular costume is retained, whereas in the Buddha figures we expect, and generally find, a monastic costume without jewelry. Starting with Yakṣa prototypes, the Bodhisattvas seem to have been developed in two directions, that of the independent figures, and that of the figures associated with the Buddha in a triad. Yakṣas as guardians, attendants, and worshippers in early Buddhist art are represented with a flower, or as *caurī*-bearers, or with folded hands; and these types appear as members of a triad long before the central figure is anthropomorphically represented. Thus, if we look at the Sāñcī north *toraṇa*, outer face, we find on the topmost architrave in the center a *Dharma-cakra* (Wheel), that is to say, the Buddha turning the Wheel of the Law, in other words preaching the first sermon at Benares; and on either side, though one is now missing, a *caurī*-bearing Yakṣa (Fig. 14). It may be noted the left hand grasps the folds of the drapery—a feature very characteristic of Buddha figures. Again, between the lowest and second architraves we see three uprights (Fig. 20), in the center a Bodhi-tree, representing the Buddha on the occasion of the Great Enlightenment, and on either side a Yakṣa holding a rose lotus. The *caurī*-bearing type persists long after the anthropomorphic image appears (Figs. 34, 35, 60) but is later on replaced by differentiated Bodhisattva types holding attributes. If however we consider the lotus-bearing type just referred to and illustrated in Figure 20, we are immediately struck by the fact that there is only one way in which they can be described, from an iconographic point of view, namely as *padmapāṇi*, that is to say, "having a rose lotus in the hand." I do not mean to assert that these figures already represent the Bodhisattva Padmapāṇi, though that may be possible; I do mean to say that when it became necessary to present this Bodhisattva to the eye, the type lay ready to hand. It may well be that the very conception of a Bodhisattva Padmapāṇi was suggested by the existence of *padmapāṇi* Yakṣas. A parallel case is that of the Yakṣa Vajrapāṇi (Figs. 35, 40), originally the Buddha's faithful attendant, later the Bodhisattva Vajrapāṇi (Fig. 65). Incidentally, this Yakṣa and Bodhisattva Vajrapāṇi should not be confused with Indra, to whom the epithet *vajrapāṇi* also applies, but who never became a Bodhisattva. Regarding the generally similar aspect of Bodhisattvas and Yakṣas little more need be said, except to remark that the resemblance of type is such that in more than one instance modern students have mistaken ancient Yakṣa figures for Bodhisattvas.[37] As regards a resemblance in function, it need scarcely be pointed out that Bodhisattvas, like Yakṣas, are frequently worshipped, not for the sake of enlightenment, but as guardians and protectors from earthly ills.[38]

In the case of Jaina iconography, the sequence is even clearer; only here there are no Bodhisattvas, and the *caurī*-bearing attendants remain to the last as attendants, well known to be Yakṣas. It is noteworthy that some of these Jaina Yakṣas, attendant on Jinas, bear the names of Hindu deities, such as Brahmā, who are not, from the usual Hindu point of view, Yakṣas at all.[39] We are reminded here of the iconographic descent of the Hindu deities, which like the Buddhist divinities are derived from a limited early

37. Cf. Diez, *Die Kunst Indiens*, fig. 131; H. P. Sastri, in *J. B. O. R. S.*, 1919, p. 552.

38. References to Yakṣas as guardian or familiar spirits will be found in Foucher, *L'art gréco-bouddhique du Gandhara*, II, 47; in the *Prabandhacintāmaṇi* of Merutunga, Tawney's translation, p. 203 (there is a corresponding passage in the *Kathākośa*; and *Mahāvaṁsa*, ch. X).

39. Glasenapp, *Der Jainismus*, pp. 361, 362. J. Burgess, *Digambara Jaina Iconography*, in *Indian Antiquary*, XXXII, 1903.

stock of types in which the Yakṣa, or king formula predominates; the two types are essentially similar—Yakṣas are by no means always represented as pot-bellied. It may indeed have been objected that some of the worshipping figures associated with symbols of Buddha in early Buddhist art are not really Yakṣas, but kings; this may be true, but only illustrates the fact that the early conception of a divine personage is based upon that of an ideal ruler (Cakravartin). This being the case, indeed, it is the less surprising that the similarity of Bodhisattva and royal types should have persisted throughout the later development; this only accords with the view, moreover, that on the one hand, kings are earthly divinities, while on the other hand divinities by their very nature are persons who exercise dominion (*aiśvarya*) over a more or less extended domain in accordance with their special functions. The phylogeny of Hindu iconography, however, lies outside the scope of the present article; I may point out merely in passing the close relation existing between such early Śiva types as that of the Guḍimallam *liṅgam* and such early Yakṣa types as those of Bhārhut and Sāñcī.

The origin of the Buddhist and Hindu feminine divinities, can be only briefly referred to. If we do not meet with them very early under their Buddhist and Hindu names, that is not to say that they were not known in the same forms but under other names at an earlier date. Forms like those of Tārā or Devī in their simplest *sāttvik* aspect, representing beautiful deep-bosomed women whose only attribute is a lotus flower held in the hand are iconographically indistinguishable from the proto-Lakṣmī so often represented in reliefs of Sāñcī and Bhārhut, on coins, for example those of Amoghabhūti and of Azes, and by early terra cottas. India forms no exception to the general rule that in all religious development it is the natural human tendency to continue the worship of the ancient forms, and even in the ancient manner, accepting at first tacitly and then as a matter of course the newer interpretations and terminology. It may well be, indeed, that the image of Tārā, as Dr. Barnett has suggested,[40] goes back to the time when Anahita, whether known by that or by some other name, was worshipped alike in Western Asia and Indo-Sumerian India.[41]

The Buddhas of Mathurā and Gandhāra are both nimbate; in the former the nimbus is simply scalloped at the edge, in the latter it is plain. That the Mathurā Buddhas are nimbate is regarded by Foucher and others as a distinctive mark of Greek influence, inasmuch as both a nimbus and rays are found in Greek art of the Alexandrian period.[42] In the first place it may be remarked that the nimbus or rays must have originated in some classic area of sun-worship, and may be older than the known Greek examples.[43] In India it

40. *J. R. A. S.*, 1926, p. 765.

41. It is true that another goddess of prosperity, Ardochṣo, to use her name as it appears on early coins, enters into the body of Indian iconography; this is probably a Hellenistic form, a western Fortune, and with her characteristic cornucopia, she can be followed far into the mediaeval imagery. But how small a part this form, to be identified by the un-Indian cornucopia, plays beside the innumerable feminine divinities, Buddhist or Hindu, who hold in their hand a lotus flower, the *līlā-kamala* of Indian poetry! As we have already remarked, it is far from our object to deny the existence of any foreign element whatever in Indian iconography; we wish only that the matter should be apprehended with a due sense of proportion.

For the early Indian terra cottas see Museum of Fine Arts *Bulletin*, No. 152, and a fuller account to appear in *Ipek*, 1928, also *A. S. I.*, *A. R.*, 1924-5, pls. XXII, XXVII.

42. Foucher, *L'art gréco-bouddhique du Gandhara*, I, p. 42.

43. So also the thunderbolt of Zeus is older than the earliest known Greek representations (Jacobsthal, *Der Blitz in der orientalischen und griechischen Kunst*, Berlin, 1906). In such cases it is simpler to regard the Indian occurrences as belonging to the common Indo-Western-Asiatic inheritance than as late borrowings; more especially

occurs on coins of Maues, c. 100 B. C., and so even if of western origin need not have any specific bearing on the Gandhāra question. But it would have been a most natural development within the Indian tradition. In Vedic ritual a golden disc was placed on the fire altar to represent the sun; it may well be that in other cases such a disk was placed behind the altar, at any rate this would naturally tend to be so in the case of smaller altars bearing cult objects. Radiance is a quality associated with all the Devas, and we might expect that when an anthropomorphic image took its place upon the altar, once empty or occupied by a symbol, the disc would remain—just as the Bodhi-tree remains behind the Vajrāsana when the visible Buddha takes his place upon it. At any rate we do in fact find representations of altars bearing symbols (the bowl relic, Fig. 22), having behind them just such a hemisphere as we might expect, with the usual scallop edge of the Kuṣāna nimbus; a similar half-disc appears (with rays) behind a seated Sūrya type (D 46 in the Mathurā Museum) of the Kuṣāna period (Fig. 44). It seems to me very likely that we have before us a direct traditional continuity. In any case, the nimbus cannot be regarded as an argument of much weight in the Gandhāra question. As I have constantly repeated and as cannot be too often repeated, the only real argument would consist in showing that the earliest Indian Buddha figures, whatever their date, resemble Gandhāra types and are not in the iconographic or stylistic tradition of the older indigenous works.

A rather constant distinction of Gandhāra from Mathurā Buddha figures appears in the form of the throne, which in Gandhāra is usually a lotus, in Mathurā, *a siṁhāsana*, that is to say, a rectangular pedestal supported by lions. The exact significance of this difference is hard to explain. It may be remarked that the Gandhāra lotus is somewhat un-Indian in that it is represented not as a broad expanded surface, but rather suggesting a prickly artichoke, as if the Indian conception of a firm and easy seance, had been somewhat misunderstood. If the Gandhāra sculptors depended wholly or partly on a literary tradition, perhaps the distinction arose in connection with the double meaning of the word *padmāsana*, which signifies both the lotus seance and the lotus seat. In India proper the sculptor would have been better aware that the Buddha could be represented in *padmāsana* (lotus seance) without necessarily being seated upon a lotus. That the Indian sculptors followed a tradition in which the lion had importance, no doubt in connection with the conception of the Tathāgata as Śākyasiṁha, the Lion of the Śākyas, is also shown by the fact that in some standing figures, for example Friar Bala's Bodhisattva, a lion is represented seated between the rather widely separated feet of the Master.

In Gandhāra Bodhisattvas, the turban, when represented, is usually of a typically Indian, Kuṣāna, form. When, as in Figures 17 and 32 we find in this headdress a Dhyāni

when we have also early literary references to the form (*Atharva Veda*, XI, 10, 3) where the *trisaṁdhi*, the three-pointed bolt of Indra, is deified (Bloomfield, *Artharva Veda* . . . p. 75). For the earliest Indian representation of a *vajra* (Maurya or Śuṅga) see *A. S. I.*, *A. R.*, 1911-12, p. 93 and pl. XXXII, 5. As regards the innumerable *motifs* such as winged lions common to Indian and Western Asiatic art, it is not only (as Fergusson long ago perceived, *Tree and Serpent Worship*, p. 132) "not clear that the Indian form may not be of an original stock as old or older than the Assyrian," but very probable that this is so, the *motifs* being cognates rather than late borrowings.

The oldest nimbus with which I am acquainted appears as a circle with flaming rays surrounding the flying deity Asur on an enameled faience from Assur now in the British Museum and dating from the ninth century B. C. (W. Andrae, *Farbige Keramik aus Assur*, Berlin, 1923, p. 13 and pl. 8). It is interesting to observe on the same plaque a representation of clouds and raindrops according to a formula later traceable in Central Asia and in India (see my *Catalogue of Indian Collections*, Boston, part V, nos. CLVIII and CCCXCIVb, pp. 120, 201).

30—Buddha

31—Buddha

32—Bodhisattva

33—Buddha

30, 32, Buddha and Bodhisattva Types, Gandhāra; 31, 33, Mathurā

34—"Bodhisattva" (Buddha) with two Attendants; Lion Throne

35—Buddha with two Attendants (Yakṣa Vajrapāṇi on Proper Right)

38—Buddha Teaching and First Meditation

36—Bodhisattva Maitreya

37—Buddha (?) with Turban

39—Buddha with two Attendants

40—Visit of Indra; Yakṣa Vajrapāṇi above

Early Mathurā Seated Buddha Type

Buddha represented, in Mathurā works in an Indian manner and in Gandhāra works in the Hellenistic tradition, it seems most natural to assume that the Indian type is original. Incidentally it may be remarked that the occurrence of this formula in the Kuṣāna period is one of the earliest plastic evidences available of an already advanced stage in the development of Mahāyāna theology. Be it observed that it is not inconceivable that such a small Buddha figure had been actually worn by Indian Buddhist kings, who might have wished to be regarded as Bodhisattvas, just as Kadphises II using the title of Maheśvara suggests that he is an incarnation of Śiva; at a much later period such a Buddha figure was certainly worn in the headdress by the Sinhalese king Vimala Dharma Sūrya.[44]

Another cycle of the same kind is represented by the *līlā kamala* or *līlābja*, lotus of dalliance, held in the hand by divinities and by kings and queens from the time of the earliest reliefs up to the present day; whether this lotus had originally a precise symbolic significance, or, as the *Mahāpadāna Sutta* expresses it, was simply "dear to and beloved of all," we can hardly say.[45]

Great differences are found too in the treatment of the hair. In Gandhāra the hair is generally thick and undulating (Fig. 30) and the *uṣṇīṣa* is either covered by the hair or replaced by a kind of chignon. In Mathurā, however, both Buddha and Jina images are represented at first with a spiral protuberance (Fig. 34) which is a lock of hair and not an *uṣṇīṣa*; later the whole head and hair are covered with small short curls, and this type after the second century becomes the almost universal rule, the only example (Fig. 61)

44. Reproduced in Rouffaer and Juynboll, *Indische Batikkunst*, and in my *Mediaeval Sinhalese Art*, pl. xxii.

45. In early Indian art the lotus is held in the hand, is used as a seat or pedestal, is represented in medallions, and in the full-vase (*puṇṇa-ghaṭa, bhadda-ghaṭa*) *motif*, and constantly employed in the decorative borders. Foucher is undoubtedly right in regarding the lotus when treated *per se* as of symbolic significance, and as designating the feminine divinity who holds the lotus in her hand and is sometimes accompanied by elephants who pour down waters upon her from jars held in their trunks. This type, exactly corresponding to the later Lakṣmī and Gaja-Lakṣmī, when met with in Buddhist art, Foucher describes as Māyā-Devī; and this goddess, or the lotus alone, he regards as designating the nativity of the Buddha. The type, however, is equally a favorite one in early Jaina art; it appears on early votive terra cottas, and on coins which we have no special reason to regard as Buddhist. Perhaps the most fully realized type is that of the pillar from the Jamālpur mound, Mathurā, now B 89 in the Lucknow Museum (Cunningham, *A. S. W. I., Reports*, I, or my *History of Indian and Indonesian Art*, fig. 74); here we have the full-vase *motif*, with masses of lotus flowers rising from it, and the goddess standing on one of the flowers amongst the others. This proto-Lakṣmī *may* have designated the nativity in some special instances, but we have no evidence that such was the case: Māyā-Devī when unmistakably represented in the later nativities belongs to the dryad (*vṛkṣakā*) type. What we may well be sure of is that fundamentally the goddess of the lotus is a figure of Abundance, drawn from the warm and living imagery of popular cults. Like the dryads and many of the railing figures, the aspect of fertility is emphasized. When the elephants are present, these are surely the life-giving monsoon clouds. And the rose lotus, which Foucher recognized as her particular symbol, is at once an emblem of the waters and of abundance.

In old Jaina texts the Gaja-Lakṣmī composition is always described as the lustration (*abhiṣekha*) of Fortune (Śrī).

The significance of the lotus seat and pedestal must be another than this. It will not be overlooked that Brahmā in the Epics is called *abjaja*, lotus-born, and *kamalāsana*, seated on a lotus. In the *Śatapatha Brāhmaṇa* (VII, 4, 1, 8 and X, 5, 2, 6) the lotus plant is said to represent the (cosmic) waters, and the earth is a lotus leaf floating on the waters. Here the idea of divine and miraculous birth is present. In later works the mysterious purity of the lotus, which springs from the mud and is yet so fair, and whose leaves though they rest on the water are not wetted by it, is often referred to. Also, it is characteristic of the gods that they do not touch the earth; the lotus flowers that rise beneath their feet and which, even in seated images, are, as it were, their footstool designate this peculiarity.

In the later cosmologies both macrocosm and microcosm are in various ways compared to a lotus, and it is possible that some conception of this kind is present when a lotus is seen in the hand of a deity; the *līlā-kamala*, lotus of dalliance, a toy as it were in human hands, is likewise the cosmic scene of the divine *līlā*.

Finally, it can hardly be doubted that at the time we are speaking of the history of decorative art was already so ancient that the lotus may well have been extensively used simply as a familiar design, without special or conscious significance.

of the smooth head dating from the Gupta period being the Māṅkuwāṛ image, 448/9 A. D. In Gandhāra, as the process of Indianization of the type proceeds, the flowing locks are restricted and by gradual transitions come to conform to the Indian curly formula. Both types, the early single spiral (Fig. 34) and the later multiplicity of short curls seem to reflect, though in different ways, the tradition of the *Nidānakathā* that when the Bodhisattva shore his locks, his hair "was reduced to two inches in length, and curling from the right, lay close to his head, and so remained as long as he lived."

The occurrence of Jaina types, practically identical with the Buddha types, except for the absence of the robe, is noteworthy. It is generally assumed, and must be assumed, when the Hellenistic theory is adopted, that the Jaina types are derived from Buddhist ones. But such little (palaeographic) evidence as is available tends to show that the Jaina type as found on *āyāgapaṭas* (votive slabs) (Figs. 41, 42) are somewhat older than any dated Buddha figures. Laufer[46] has suggested with some plausibility that Jainas preceded the Buddhists in the adoption of an iconolatrous cult.

It is a rather mysterious fact that though the Jainas, like the Buddhists, were well established in Taxila in the Scytho-Parthian period, as architectural remains prove, not a single example of Graeco-Jain sculpture appears either then or at any subsequent period.

A few sculptures that may be called Graeco-Hindu are known, but these belong to the later period (third century) when Gandhāra art is much Indianized. The most interesting of these figures is a three-headed Maheśa (so-called Trimūrti) from Chārsada,[47] comparable to the three-headed Śiva with the bull on one of the coin types of Vāsudeva.[48] This Maheśa type can be traced across Central Asia (possibly in the sense of a Lokeśvara) and to China and Japan.[49] In the same way a Buddha type of Mathurā origin can be followed through Turkestan to China.[50]

The Buddha and Jina (Fig. 43) type of a seated or standing figure, sheltered by the expanded hoods of a polycephalous Nāga, and the similar Hindu type (Viṣṇu-Anantaśayin—but not always reclining, there being a fine seated example in the Vaiṣṇava Cave at Bādāmī) present a common interest. Here in the same way it would be usual to derive the Hindu from the Buddhist type; but the converse is more probable. At any rate the *Mahābhārata* story of Rāja Adi in which the sleeping Droṇa is found sheltered by a serpent's hoods is older than any possible Buddha figure. From this story is derived the place name Ahichatra, "serpent-umbrella," and, as Cunningham suggests, the Buddhists probably took over the idea from the Hindus.[51] There is a close resemblance between

46. Laufer, *Das Citralakṣaṇa*, p. 18.

47. Natesa Aiyar, *Trimurti Image in the Peshawar Museum*, in *A. S. I., A. R.*, 1913-14.

48. R. B. Whitehead, *Catalogue of the Coins in the Panjab Museum*, pl. XX, 11; Gardner, *Coins of the Greek and Scythic Kings . . .*, pl. XXIX, 10; another good specimen is in Boston.

49. Stein, *Ancient Khotan*, pl. LX; Chavannes, *Mission archéologique dans la Chine septentrionale*, pl. 224; and appearing in Japan as Dai Itoku.

50. Foucher, *L'art gréco-bouddhique du Gandhara*, fig. 563; Stein, *Ancient Khotan*, pl. LXXXII; Sirén, *Chinese Sculpture*, pp. xxxvii f. (the affinity of style of a great number of Chinese sculptures from the end of the fifth to the beginning of the following century "is so evident and uniform that it hardly needs to be pointed out in detail," and if this is ignored by Foucher, it is because he "made it his task to trace the influence of Gandhāra in as many places as possible"), xli, lxvi, and pls. 116, 117, also *Documents d'art chinois*, pls. XLIX, LIV, LVI (Indian treatment of the hair).

51. *A. S. W. I., Reports*, I, pp. 255, 256. Ahichatra is one of the places where a stupa, traditionally of Aśoka, was erected by the side of a Nāga tank (Beal, *Buddhist Records of the Western World*, p. 200).

It may be added that, as is well known, modern standing figures consisting of a human figure with serpent hoods rising from the back between the shoulders, are known as Baldeo (Balarāma); but Balarāma in the *Mahābhārata* is identified with Sesa Nāga, and is described as having his head wreathed with snakes (Hopkins, *Epic Mythology*, p. 212). It is possible therefore that the iconography is ancient, and not the result of a modern confusion of types.

41 42

Two Ayāgapaṭas with Seated Jinas in the Centers (Mathurā)

43—*Pārśvanātha (Mathurā)*

44—*Sūrya (Mathurā)*

45—*Yakṣa with Purse (Mathurā)*

46—*Nāga with Attendants (Amarāvatī)*

47—*Yakṣa (Deoriyā)*

Early Jina Types, Yakṣas, etc.

48—Bodhisattva Maitreya (Mathurā)

49—Nāga with Flask (Mathurā)

50—Bodhisattva (Mathurā)

51—Buddha (Mathurā)

52—Buddha (Mathurā)

Budda, Bodhisattva, and Nāga Types (Mathurā)

the appearance which would be presented by a seated polycephalous Nāga of the Mathurā or Sāñcī[52] type, and a seated Buddha or Jina sheltered by a Nāga, the only difference being that in the one case the hoods rise from the back between the shoulders, in the other the coiled tail of the Nāga forms a seat, and its whole body is really quite distinct from that of the principal figure. There *may* be a genetic connection here. The polycephalous Nāga is very rarely met with in Gandhāra.

If the Indian Buddha figure, Mathurā type, is not derived from Gandhāra, what is the relation between the two schools, that is to say, in the beginning and during the period preceding the stylistic Indianization of the Gandhāra school? Exactly to what extent Gandhāra iconography is derived from preëxisting Indian forms, either through Mathurā or otherwise, is still a matter for further research. Certainly some Gandhāra sculptures are replicas, or very closely related developments, of preëxisting Indian ones. When Spooner remarks[53] of a Bodhisattva fragment found at Takht-i-Bāhī, "The resemblance of this figure to some of the Bhārhut sculpture is remarkable, but of course this can only be accidental," the "of course" seems to be dictated by a preconceived view. The resemblance is not accidental in the case of the *Vessantara Jātaka*[54] compositions (Fig. 57), or in that of the Gandhāra Vṛkṣakā types (woman-and-tree). M. Foucher, indeed, has himself shown to what an extent Gandhāra made use of older Indian formulae.[55] How far this was also true in the case of the Buddha figure needs further investigation. I by no means positively assert that Buddha figures were first made in Mathurā and afterwards copied in Gandhāra, though as Goloubew says, that is possible. The Gandhāra school may have been based, like the Northern Wei school in China, mainly on literary traditions. Stylistically, of course, Gandhāra is independent; but hardly more definitely so than China or even Java, and Chinese or Javanese style are no proof of Chinese or Javanese origins. All we can say definitely is that practically every element essential to the iconography of Buddha and Bodhisattva figures appears in early Indian art before the Buddha figure of Gandhāra or Mathurā is known.

5. STYLE AND CONTENT: DIFFERENTIATION OF INDIAN AND HELLENISTIC TYPES

In the previous chapter only the iconographic elements (theme and shape) have been referred to; it remains to point out that the Indian stylistic sequence presents a similar continuity, and to define the distinction of the Indian from the Hellenistic types in respect of content and form.

In the Pārkham and Deoriyā images (Figs. 2, 3) we have works of archaic aspect, characterized by frontality and an abrupt transition from the plane of the chest to that of the sides; in the Patna image (Fig. 3) the same features are equally evident. These archaic features, of course, are gradually refined upon as time passes. More significant and permanent is the great plastic voluminousness; everything is felt in mass, and nothing

52. As at Sāñcī, Fergusson, *Tree and Serpent Worship*, pl. XXIV, 1 and 2.

53. Spooner, *Excavations at Takht-i-Bahi*, in *A. S. I., A. R.*, 1907-08, with reference to fig. 6, *ibid.*

54. Cf. also another Gandhāra example, *A. S. I., A. R.*, 1909-10, pl. XVIII. If the Bhārhut relief had been lost, it would surely have been claimed that this composition originated in Gandhāra; and, in fact, Sir Aurel Stein takes this for granted (*Desert Cathay*, I, p. 489). The same composition occurs in a Miran fresco of the second or third century A. D. (Stein, *op. cit.*), and survives in modern Buddhist art (see my *Mediaeval Sinhalese Art*, frontispiece).

55. *L'art gréco-bouddhique du Gandhara*, I, pp. 206 ff.

in outline; this quality is maintained in Indian sculpture until after the Gupta period, while it is the very opposite of what we find in Gandhāra, where sculpture represents the decadence of a tradition, and is, as we should naturally expect, attenuated and linear. The early Indian figures stand symmetrically, with the feet somewhat apart, and this is also the case with later images of the type of Friar Bala's Bodhisattva (Fig. 2). In the early figures the sculptor has at his command an adequate scheme for the representation of the folds of drapery; and this drapery clings closely to the figure. In many Śuṅga and early Andhra works the body is revealed almost as though it were nude. Here again is a feature that is highly characteristic of the early Mathurā Buddhist figures, and of Gupta art generally. In Gandhāra the drapery is treated realistically, the folds rising well above the level of those parts of the material that are actually in contact with the flesh; at Mathurā the treatment is schematic and clinging.

Nothing is more characteristic of the early Indian art than its affirmative force; the Gandhāra style by comparison is listless. This radiation of force is scarcely at all reduced in the Mathurā standing and seated figures, which in this respect, indeed, are somewhat at variance with the dispassionate serenity which we are apt to regard as characteristic of Buddha types. In the early Indian works and up to the end of the second century A. D. there is hardly ever to be found deliberate grace; it is not without reason, though the language may sound strange in the ears of students of art, that some archaeologists have described the Gandhāra figures as graceful, the Mathurā types as clumsy and unwieldy. This only expresses the common and unsophisticated view that regards all early art as "awkward," and all late art as "better;" but in the present connection it serves to exhibit very well the stylistic gulf that separates Gandhāra from Mathurā. In fact the Gandhāra types, like other Hellenistic works, are soft and woolly; those of Mathurā, tense, and even strained. Whatever we may think about the iconography, it would be impossible to imagine a genetic connection of either school with the other in point of style.

Again, the earlier Indian types are products, not of observation, but of cerebration; they are mental abstractions. As Indian culture became more conscious, racial taste was more and more a determining factor in such abstractions. That the model upon which the artist worked was regarded from the standpoint of knowledge, and not of observation, is reflected in the use of *sādhanās* or *dhyāna mantrams*, which constitute the main part of the *śilpa śāstras* so far as they are concerned with the making of cult images. No natural form is imitated merely because it is present in nature; on the contrary, all the formulae of art are as much *saṁskṛtam* as Sanskrit itself, and every phrase was intended to have a definite significance. Of course, the art as it develops, comes to have an appearance of greater "truth to nature;" the actuality and spontaneity of the Ajaṇṭā paintings, for example, have been remarked upon. But it would be an error to suppose that even here we have an unsophisticated art, like that of those who take nature for their model. The Indian theory of knowledge, as M. Masson-Oursel has pointed out[56] amounts to this, that objects are created by thought, not that preëxisting objects are perceived. Hence the importance of correct thought; and this in relation to art is theoretically a matter of revelation, and secondarily, one of tradition. The forms created by correct thought need

56. *Notes sur l'esthetique indienne* in *Revue des arts asiatique*, III, 1926. Cf. also Zimmer, *Kunstform und Yoga*, 1926—"*Kultbild ist Yantra.*"

not by any necessity conform to those perceived in nature by untrained perception; all that is necessary is that they should be consistent and significant.

Where we think we recognize an increasing "truth to nature" and assume a closer observation, as in the Ajaṇṭā paintings referred to, what we have in reality is greater consciousness;[57] the artist, *mehr einfühlende*, is more aware of the tensions that he represents, and consequently represents them more convincingly. But the corresponding gestures had already been codified in dictionaries of gesture (Bharata's *Nāṭya Śāstra*); and the painter is really using a highly artificial and conventional language of glances, inclinations, and gestures, all with definite significance. When we come to examine his supposed realism more closely, we find that it has no foundation in the observation of anatomy or modeling, and that it depends entirely on an understanding of the psychology of gesture. When later on the same formulae have become rigid habits, this only means that the race has fallen from the high level of consciousness and subtlety that marked the zenith of its culture, not that observation of nature has been abandoned; the suggestion of realism is immediately lost, which is by no means the case in decadent Greek art.

Śilpa śāstras were certainly current in the Gupta period; Hsüan Tsang refers to such works as forming a section of the *Śāstras* studied by laymen.[58] But the use of formulae goes back to a much earlier time. Indians from the beginning were deeply interested in physiognomy, and it is with this preoccupation that a fundamental type like that of the Mahāpuruṣa-Cakravartin was conceived. This theoretical type, with its thirty-two principal marks (*lakṣaṇas*) and other minor marks, is older than the Buddha image, older presumably than the Buddha himself. At least, the Buddha is described as a Mahāpuruṣa in canonical books, and as possessing these marks, of which some are represented in the sculptures. Thus the Buddhist had taken over at an early period from non-Buddhist sources a conception of the Buddha as Mahāpuruṣa or Cakravartin; the *lakṣaṇas* were certainly not the invention of Buddhists, but were taken over by them and applied to the person of the Master. In other words, a definite idea of the Buddha's appearance existed before the time of actual representations; nor did this idea differ from that which a Hindu would have had of the appearance of such a god as Viṣṇu, likewise a Mahāpuruṣa.[59] That the Buddha could not be regarded as a man in the ordinary sense of the word may be gathered from the words attributed to himself, in reply to the questions of Droṇa, a Brāhman who found him seated at the foot of a tree; was he a Deva, Gandharva, Yakṣa, or man? The Master replies that he is none of these, but a Buddha.[60] Like the gods, he is anthropomorphic, but not a man; and as a deity he stands with them as a fit and natural subject for iconographic representation.

57. The case of painting is not quite the same as that of the religious sculpture. Painting was to some extent cultivated as a fine art and as an accomplishment. Portraits must certainly have been likenesses. In sculpture, even the effigies of donors are types, rather than likenesses. The sculptor should represent the gods, as Śukrācārya says, not men—though the latter may be pleasing, it is not the way to heaven (*Śukranītisāra*, IV, iv, 154-157). It is significant that a knowledge of the science of dancing was considered essential to the understanding of painting (*Viṣṇudharmottaram*, III, II, 3).

58. As stated in the *Si yu ki*, Beal, *Buddhist Records of the Western World*, I, p. 78.

59. On the subject of the Mahāpuruṣa, see Laufer, *Das Citralakṣaṇa*, pp. 14 ff.; Grünwedel, *Buddhist Art in India*, pp. 80, 120 ff., 133; Kern, *Manual of Indian Buddhism*, pp. 62, 95; other references, Beal, *Buddhist Records of the Western World*, I, p. 1; R. O. Francke, *Der dogmatische Buddha nach dem Dighanikáya*, *W. Z. K. M.*, 28, 1924.

60. *Anguttara Nikāya*, II, 37. Cf. *Lalita Vistara*, ch. xvi, "Is this Brahmā, Indra, or Vaiśravaṇa, or some mountain deity?"

All this mentality and formulation are foreign to the Hellenistic tradition, which represents the last term of a long development that had been determined by a profound interest in human form studied for its own sake. Greek idealism regarded even ideal forms as objective realities, not as fashioned by thought; hence, or in other words, Greek instinct was perceptive and outwardly directed. Even though the story be a myth, it is still significant that a Greek sculptor should have been supposed to have created a perfect type by combining the beauties of five different individuals. An Indian, connoisseur of the beauty of women as he was, would never have resorted to models, because he knew *a priori* in what the beauty of women consisted, or if we can imagine him in doubt, would have consulted a *śāstra*; it would never have occurred to him to find out what it was by turning to nature. The Greeks, like Wordsworth, though not perhaps in quite the same way, were "fond of nature;" and this kind of art they brought to perfection. But while the Indian kind of art in its decadence becomes a repetition of stereotyped formulae no longer felt, the Greek kind in its decadence becomes rhetorical and facile.

We are dealing, in fact, not merely with two different kinds of art, but with two arts in entirely different stages of their development; the Greek already decadent, the Indian still primitive. A serious stylistic influence of a realistic or decadent art upon a formal or primitive art (and we have seen that both distinctions held) could only have been destructive; we have seen too much of the influence of European art on Asiatic art within the last hundred years not to be aware of this; nothing inwardly resembling Gandhāra art had been produced in India before the nineteenth century. The fact that art of the Indian school pursued a normal course (i. e., it "develops") from first to last is not a proof that the refinement of the primitive types was due to external influences, but a proof of continuity in the indigenous tradition.

Apparently only one example of Mathurā sculpture in the round representing a Buddha or Bodhisattva has been regarded as an actual imitation of a Gandhāra prototype:[61] and only one piece of actual Gandhāra sculpture has been found in Mathurā.[62] It is admitted by all students and will be obvious from the most cursory examination of the accompanying illustrations that the sculptures of Kaniṣka's reign differ so much from Gandhāra types that a genetic connection seems inconceivable.[63] It is only in certain reliefs mostly of the middle period (Vāsudeva and later), as justly noted by Codrington,[64] that Gandhāra influence can be definitely recognized (Figs. 58, 59). The Dhruv Tīlā stupa drum[65] described by Foucher as a "*caricature lamentablement indianisée*"[66] must be reckoned amongst these.

Why did not the Mathurā craftsman adopt more freely Hellenistic mannerisms? I think it was mainly because the required types lay ready to hand in the local tradition. The transition from a Buddha type like that of the Ujjain coin (Fig. 9) to a designated Go(tama) Boydo (the legend of Kaniṣka's seated Buddha coin), and from a *padmapāṇi*

61. A 47 in the Mathurā Museum, Vogel, in *A. S. I., A. R.*, 1906-07, p. 15.

62. F 42 in the Mathurā Museum, Burgess, *Ancient Monuments*, pls. 56, 57.

63. See my *Indian Origin of the Buddha Image, J. A. O. S.*, XLVI, p. 169.

64. *Ancient India*, p. 47.

65. V. A. Smith, *The Jain Stupa of Mathurā*, pls. CV-CVII.

66. In *J. A.*, X, 11, 1903, p. 323.

attendant to an attendant Padmapāṇi took place almost unnoticed. That which seems to us a kind of artistic revolution really implied no new iconographic invention; it involved a new terminology much more than a new art. India had long been familiar with images of gods; Patañjali, presumably in the second century B. C., speaks of images of Śiva, Skandha, and Viśākha, not to mention other and earlier indications and the known Yakṣa figures. The whole process belongs to the theistic development which had been taking place, and is naturally reflected in the substitution of anthropomorphic figures for the older abstract symbolism. Buddhism cannot be considered alone; that Buddha had come to be regarded as Devatideva, God of gods, shows that, as usual, each religion is affected by the current tendency. There is no canonical proscription of images in Buddhist literature, early or late; and very soon the Buddhist authors take it for granted that images had been made even in the Buddha's own lifetime.

Mathurā sculptors, then, had no more occasion to adopt the Hellenistic iconography or style than they had to replace their own Brāhmī by Kharoṣṭhī, which must have been the official script of Kaniṣka's capitals at Peshāwar and Kapiśa. I do not believe that the slightest prejudice against Gandhāra art, as such, existed; or if so, only as an instinctive taste, the nature of which is indicated in Le Coq's just remark: "*Allen Asiaten erscheinen Europaergesichter (also auch die der Hellenen) sehr unschön.*"[67] I once showed to a Kandyan craftsman, a descendant of *śilpins* and *ācāryas*, and proficient in his art, a good example of European design, rather thinking he would admire it; in fact, however, he seemed neither attracted nor repelled, and merely remarked, "*Ek eka raṭa, ek eka veḍa,*" that is, "every country has its own style." I believe that a Mathurā craftsman would have regarded a Gandhāra work in the same way.

It must be remembered too that Buddhist and Hindu images were not regarded and never have been regarded in India as works of art; they were made as means of edification. Prestige attached to sanctity, not to style; the same situation may be observed in modern times in connection with such relatively uncouth types as those of the Śrī Nātha-jī[68] of Nāthadvār and Jagannātha of Purī, of which painted replicas are constantly made, adhering rigidly to type, regardless of the availability of much more attractive (humanly speaking) Kṛṣṇa and Viṣṇu types. The modern imager is totally unaware of stylistic degeneration; in the same way he must in early times have been unaware of the virtue of his art. He did not think at all in terms of our connoisseurship; the plastic style of his day came to him as naturally as the spoken language, and both as a matter of course. Particular images would only be copied on account of their special sanctity, not because of their artistic merits.[69] Particular places would only become centers of distribution, as Mathurā was, or as Jaipur still is, because the religious importance and prosperity of such places during an extended period had necessitated the existence there of ateliers, able to

67. *Bilderatlas zur Kunst und Kunstgeschichte Mittelasiens*, p. 28. Cf. Lafcadio Hearn, *About Faces in Japanese Art*, in *Gleanings in Buddha Fields*.

68. It is perhaps worth while to remark here that the image of Śrī Nātha-jī which was found underground near Mathurā, and subsequently removed to Nāthadvāra near Udaipur, still the main sanctuary of the Vallabhācāryas, may well be in fact a Kuṣāṇa Buddha. The image, so far as I know, has never been photographed or published, but the painted replicas show a standing figure, with the left hand on the hip, and the right raised in *abhaya mudrā*, with a certain angularity suggestive of early Mathurā types. This would not be by any means an isolated instance of the later worship of an old Mathurā Buddhist figure under the name of a Hindu deity.

69. In this fact there is nothing peculiar to Indian psychology: the same has held good from first to last in the history of Christian iconographic art.

supply the needs of the devout inhabitants or pilgrims. Now we know that in the time of Kaniṣka Mathurā was a most important Buddhist center, probably the most important in India; as remarked by Przyluski[70] in quite another connection, "*Mathurā eût parmi les communautés bouddhiques une situation privilegée;*" and it played a very great part in the dissemination of the faith. This being so, it is not in the least surprising that the Mathurā school should have played such an important part as it did in the history of Buddhist art.[71]

We are able, moreover, to trace the influence of the Mathurā types, not only at Amarāvatī, but as the formative basis of Gupta art, by means of archaeological data, and not only by stylistic evidence. In the time of Kaniṣka Mathurā had already such a reputation that Buddha and Bodhisattva images were exported thence to Sāñcī, Prayāg, Amīn (near Thanesar), Kasiā, Śrāvastī, Pāṭaliputra, Sārnāth, Bodhgayā, Rājagṛha, and to many parts of the Panjāb, including even Taxila. At Sārnāth, copies of Mathurā types have been definitely recognized. In the Gupta period, while local ateliers had developed at places like Sārnāth and Sāñcī, Mathurā sculptures were still exported to these and other sites. These facts sufficiently explain the close relation of the Kuṣāna and Gupta forms.

Gupta art bears within itself the proof of its Indian origins. As Dr. Laufer has remarked, one has no need of the panoply of anthropology to recognize that the Buddha types of Ajaṇṭā are representations of true Indians, and have no connection with the sculpture of Gandhāra; they are "*echt indisch und haben keinen Gandhara-geruch.*"[72] This is only what has been remarked by Vincent Smith, Goloubew, and Foucher himself, in connection with the sculpture.[73] The Gupta type is a normal and direct development of the Mathurā type; and this Gupta type is the dominating model underlying all those of Farther India and Indonesia. We have only to look at a sequence of examples beginning with the Pārkham image (Fig. 2) and culminating in the Mathurā types of the Gupta period (Fig. 5) to realize that there is no room at any point in the development for the intercalation of any model based on Hellenistic tradition. If such an influence was exerted, and to some extent it can be recognized in the middle Kuṣāna period, it was so slight and ephemeral as to have become unrecognizable within a century, or at the most within two centuries.

70. J. Przyluski, *Aśokāvadāna*, 1923, p. 9.

71. A fact more than once emphasized by Vogel (in *A. S. I., A. R.*, 1909-10, p. 78, and *Catalogue Mathurā Museum*, p. 28), who can only have regarded it as "not a little curious" because of his preconviction that it should have been not Mathurā, but Gandhāra, that exercised a great influence on Buddhist art in other parts of India.

72. Laufer, *Das Citralakṣaṇa*, p. 16.

73. References to the statements made in this and the preceding paragraph will be found in my *Indian Origin of the Buddha Image*, in *J. A. O. S.*, XLVI, 1926. In addition, Foucher, *L'art gréco-bouddhique du Gandhara*, p. 611: "*ce sont les répliques de Mathurā qui ont servi de modèle à Bénarès, et ce sont les répliques de Bénarès que le Magadha a copiées a son tour . . . Son évolution . . . se traduit encore et toujours par l'élimination progressive de l'élément étranger sous la pression du goût indigène*"; and Sahni, *Guide to Sārnāth*, 1926 ed., p. 11: "The arrival of this (Friar Bala's) statue at Sārnāth must have been so welcome that local artists at once set to work and the Sārnāth Museum contains two statues (Ba 2 and 3) which are almost exact copies of the one from Mathurā. Vincent Smith goes so far as to say that "The style of the Sārnāth works (of Kusāna date) is so closely related to that of Mathurā that illustrations may be dispensed with." The Sārnāth types of Buddha and Bodhisattva images which followed are rightly regarded as the finest creations of the Gupta period. It was no wonder therefore, that this new art so rapidly spread not only to the rest of India, but also to the neighboring countries of Siam, Cambodia, and Ceylon." It will be seen that *all* that is required to establish a Hellenistic origin of the Buddha image as it appears in the Gupta period, fully evolved, is to show that Friar Bala's Bodhisattva type (Fig. 4) is a "*réplique*" of the Gandhāra type (e. g., Fig. 53). When this has been done, I shall be ready to accept the Greek theory, bag and baggage.

6. DATING OF GANDHĀRA AND MATHURĀ BUDDHAS

Here we know nothing for certain; and what we do not know cannot be used with much cogency in support of any argument. Nor can the question of dates, whatever discoveries may be in store for us, ever by itself provide us with a final solution of our problem. For, if the Gandhāra Buddhas could be proved older than any Mathurā ones, this would not alter the admitted fact that the conception of the figure is Indian, nor the equally obvious fact that the earliest Indian Buddha figures are in stylistic and iconographic continuity with the older indigenous art. Nor, on the other hand, if priority could be proved for the Mathurā types would it alter the fact that the Gandhāra types are Hellenistic in style; the iconography in Gandhāra might still have been derived from elements already present in early Indian art, or constructed from literary sources, and a Mathurā origin of the Buddha image *in Gandhāra* would not be proven. Nor would it alter the fact that a considerable element of Hellenistic style can be followed across Central Asia into China, Korea, and Japan, nor the fact that even in India definite traces of the Gandhāran influence can be detected. Nevertheless, it will be worth while to recapitulate the few available facts, and refer to some of the conclusions that have been or may be drawn from them.

Advocates of the Hellenistic theory assume, and probably rightly, that the best works are the earliest, and, further, opine that the Gandhāra school, so far as the earliest Buddha figures are concerned, developed in the first century B. C. The Bīmarān reliquary excavated by Masson in Afghanistan before 1840 has been assigned to the first century B. C. on account of coins of Azes associated with it;[74] but methods of excavation nearly ninety years ago were not by any means as critical as they are now, coins in any case merely provide a *terminus post quem*, and Wilson himself was of the opinion that the stupas of Afghanistan "are undoubtedly all subsequent to the Christian era."[75] Marshall dates the reliquary about the beginning of the Christian era; of Gandhāra sculptures in general he remarks more cautiously that "it may be safely asserted that a number of them . . . are anterior to the reign of Kaniṣka."[76] From the inferior workmanship and *deja stéreotypée* character of the Buddha figures on the Kaniṣka reliquary (Fig. 56), made by Agesila subsequent to 120 A. D. (the date of Kaniṣka's accession here assumed, *vide infra*), Foucher and others have concluded that the period of the finest work must be pushed back to the first century B. C.[77] This is a rather bold inference to draw from the inferior workmanship of a single object, even though it would seem that it must have been one of importance. Marshall holds that "considerations of style do not permit us to determine the chronological sequence with any approach to accuracy."[78]

Three dated Gandhāra figures have been found; but it is not known to what era the dates refer. On the assumptions that have been made, the date of a standing figure from Loriyān Tangai is 6 A. D.[79] and that of a standing figure, and of a pedestal with a seated

74. Bachofer, *Zur Datierung der Gandhara Plastik*, p. 14 ("*keine zweifel zu, das es in die Zeit des Azes I gehört*").

75. *Ariana Antiqua*, p. 322.

76. *Cambridge History of India*, I, p. 648; *Guide to Taxila*, p. 60.

77. *L'art gréco-bouddhique du Gandhara*, II, p. 443; Spooner, in *A. S. I., A. R.*, 1908-09, p. 50.

78. *Guide to Taxila*, p. 31; *Cambridge History of India*, I, p. 648.

79. Bachofer, *op. cit.;* Vogel, *Inscribed Gandhara Sculptures*, in *A. S. I., A. R.*, 1903-04. Foucher assigns the date 4 B. C. If we assume the Vikrama era which is used on the Dharmarājikā silver scroll (Marshall, *Guide to Taxila*, p. 52), the date Samvat 318 becomes equivalent to c. 262 A. D. Fleet, in *J. R. A. S.*, 1913, p. 999, points out that a use of the Śaka era would make the date 396 A. D. It will be realized that the selection of eras in the various interpretations of Gandhāra Buddha image dates is often *tendenziös*.

figure, both from Haṣṭnagar, 72 A. D.[80] The Bodhisattva illustrated in Fig. 55 is not dated, but is assigned by Bachofer to the third quarter of the first century A. D. More reliable than any of these doubtful cases is the very definite negative evidence provided by scientific excavations at Taxila. Here the Scytho-Parthian and early Kuṣāna strata at the Dharmarājikā site have not yielded a single fragment of Graeco-Buddhist sculpture.[81] At Sirkap, the city in occupation at Taxila from the second century B. C. to the time of Wima Kadphises, c. 75-80 A. D., not a single piece of Graeco-Buddhist sculpture appears in the long list of finds;[82] the only sculpture of any kind in Gandhāra stone is a small figure in the round of a semi-nude goddess holding a lotus flower, quite an old Indian type, and in style intermediate between Indian and Hellenistic. The terra cotta and stucco heads from the apsidal Buddhist temple include no Buddhas or Bodhisattvas. This is very significant negative evidence, and seems to indicate that Gandhāra Buddha figures can hardly have been made until a little before the time of Kaniṣka. All that we can be quite sure of is that the Gandhāra school of Buddhist sculpture was most productive in the time of Kaniṣka, a point on which almost all authorities are agreed.[83]

The date of Kaniṣka is not yet a fact established beyond dispute; datings have ranged from 58 B. C. to the third century A. D., the substantial controversy being between those who support the date 78 A. D. and those who support the date 120 or 125 A. D. The date c. 120 A. D. adopted here is regarded by Marshall as proved by the results of excavation, and has been accepted by Vincent Smith and Sten Konow. The point is not essential to our study, where the relative dating alone is of significance.

Friar Bala's Bodhisattva at Sārnāth is dated in the third year of Kaniṣka, thus c. 123 A. D. The Kaṭrā Bodhisattva and Aṇyor Buddha from Mathurā have inscriptions palaeographically similar, and must be of the same period. A large number of other Buddha figures from Mathurā, some in the round, others in relief, are identical in style and must be dated near the same time; some are probably a little earlier than Kaniṣka, most of the others of this type assignable to his reign or that of Huviṣka. We are certainly not entitled to assume that Friar Bala's figure or any of the other figures in our possession was the first of its kind ever made. Nor is it conceivable that an image exported to Sārnāth, not to mention those of Mathurā origin found at other sites, should have been one of the

80. Bachofer; Vogel, *loc. cit.* It should be noted that the former takes Kaniṣka's date as 78 A. D., and using the 1904 edition of Vincent Smith's *Early History of India* fails to observe that Smith since returned to the date 120 A. D., in agreement with Marshall and Konow. Smith (in *J. A. S. B.*, 1889) assigned the Haṣṭnagar pedestal to the fourth century A. D., and this dating would in fact hold good if we assume the era of Azes, the numeral of the actual inscription being 384. Fleet, in *J. R. A. S.*, 1913, p. 999, uses the Vikrama era, making the date 343 A. D.

81. Marshall, in *A. S. I., A. R.*, 1912-13, pt. I, p. 12.

82. For lists of Sirkap finds, see Marshall, *Guide to Taxila*, ch. VI, and *Excavations at Taxila*, in *A. S. I., A. R.*, 1912-13, 1914-15, 1919-20.

For the Sirkap statuette see *A. S. I., A. R.*, 1919-20, p. 20 and pl. IX; and cf. the same type in Egypt, a terra cotta of about the beginning of the Christian era, Berstl, *op. cit.*, p. 173 and pl. 103, 2. The type recurs on the Limarowka vase and in other places cited by E. Herzfeld, *Die Malereien von Samarra* (*abb.* 5, etc.).

The absence of Buddhist and Jaina sculpture at Sirkap is the more striking as the architectural remains prove Buddhism and Jainism to have been flourishing.

83. Foucher, *L'art gréco-bouddhique du Gandhara*, I, p. 42; Vogel, *op. cit.*, p. 258; Smith, *History of Fine Art in India and Ceylon*, p. 132; Grünwedel, *Buddhistische Kunst in Indien*, 2nd ed., 1920, p. xiv. During the third and fourth centuries A. D. the Gandhāra school continued to flourish abundantly, but the stone is largely replaced by terra cotta and stucco, and the type becomes thoroughly Indianized (see Marshall, *Stūpa and Monastery of Jauliāñ*, in *Mem. A. S. I.*, VII, 1921). The monasteries seem to have been destroyed and the activity of the school brought to an end by the Hūṇa invasions at the end of the fifth century.

53—Buddha

54—Buddha Teaching

55—Bodhisattva

56—Kaniṣka's Reliquary (Peshāwar)

57—Vessantara Jātaka

58—Six Scenes from Life of Buddha

59—Two Scenes from Life of Buddha

53-57—Gandhāra Types; 58, 59—Reliefs from Mathurā Showing Some Gandhāra Features

60—Buddha with two Attendants (Yakṣas), Amarāvatī School

61—Buddha (Māṅkuwāṛ)

62—Buddha (Sāñcī)

63—Buddha (Sāñcī)

64—Jina (Mathurā)

65—Bodhisattva Vajrapāṇi (Ceylon)

66—Buddha (Nepal)

67—Pārśvanātha (Kannaḍa)

Buddha, Jina, and Bodhisattva Types

first Buddha images ever made; however quickly the fashion developed, however great the prestige of the Mathurā ateliers may already have been, some time must have elapsed between the first acceptance of the type in Mathurā and the development of a general demand for Mathurā Buddha images at other and distant sites throughout the Ganges valley. These considerations compel us to suppose that Buddha images must have been made in Mathurā soon after the middle of the first century A. D., at least before the end of the century.

It should be observed that the Jaina *āyāgapaṭas* from Mathurā bearing Jina figures of the same type as that of the seated Buddha figures have Brāhmī inscriptions which seem to be pre-Kuṣāna; that they were dated by Bühler in the first century B. C. depended, however, on an earlier dating of Kaniṣka than that now adopted. A reëxamination of the inscriptions is needed; all that we can say is that these slabs may well be assigned provisionally to the middle of the first century A. D.[84]

As regards the Buddha figure on an Ujjain coin (Fig. 9) I see no reason at present to date this before the first century A. D.; the fact that a coin of the same class and character bears a figure of a three-headed Maheśa, notwithstanding that it has been assigned to the second century B. C.,[85] is in itself evidence that the general type should be assigned to the first or even the second century A. D.

The so-called Buddha figures on the coins of Maues and Kadapha (Kadphises I) are indeed dateable, and the former would take us back to the beginning of the first century B. C. As stated above, however, I do not think that these can be accepted as Buddha figures; all that they certainly show is a type closely related to that of the seated Buddha figure when it finally appears and can be recognized without possibility of error.

It will be seen from what has been said above that the whole evidence for the dating of Gandhāra Buddha types in the first century B. C. or early first century A. D. rests upon five objects, of which three are dated in unknown eras, one excavated nearly a hundred years ago is dated on the evidence of coins alone, and one is of the Kaniṣka period. This is a very slender foundation upon which to base an argument flatly at variance with the evidence of the excavations at Taxila. The balance of real evidence tends to show that the Buddha figure came into general use somewhat before the beginning of the reign of Kaniṣka, and not more than fifty years at most, if so much, before his accession. The evidence is not sufficiently precise to warrant us in forming a theory as to the priority of either school. I am inclined to presume on general grounds a priority for Mathurā; but that is not evidence. All that we can assert is that the earliest Buddha types in each area are in the local style; and that later on, though some mutual influence was felt, the outstanding character of the development is one of stylistic Indianization in Gandhāra, and one of adherence to the Mathurā type in the Ganges valley, subject to the normal stylistic

84. See p. 304 above. Many of these *āyāgapaṭas* are illustrated by Vincent Smith, *The Jain Stūpa of Mathurā.*

One of the slabs from the Kaṅkālī Tīlā is dated in the reign of Śoḍāsa and is thus pre-Kuṣāna, but it is hardly safe to assume that the slabs with Jina figures are of the same age.

85. The Maheśa is illustrated by Cunningham, *Coins of Ancient India*, pl. X, 6. Rapson, *Indian Coins*, p. 14, justly remarks that there does not exist sufficient evidence to arrange the early Ujjain coins in chronological order. The ascription of the Maheśa type to the second century B. C. will be found in the *Cambridge History of India*, p. 532, the coin being again illustrated in pl. V, 19. But no polycephalous type is certainly older than the reign of Vāsudeva, and it is impossible to date the Ujjain coin before the second century A. D.

evolution which marks the transition from Kusāna to Gupta types. Great scorn has been poured upon the view that Gupta art would have been just what it is had the Graeco-Buddhist school of Gandhāra never existed, and of course such a statement could not be literally defended; yet I am prepared to assert that the Hellenistic element actually traceable in Gupta art is really insignificant. In view of the considerations and facts brought forward above, it becomes impossible to treat the phrase "Greek origin of the Buddha image" as representing anything more than a rhetorical misuse of language; if art of the Gandhāra school, as its students admit, is half Indian, art of the Kuṣāna and Gupta periods in the Ganges valley is altogether Indian, for it deals with the same ideas, and uses a plastic language that is in direct continuity with that of the preceding centuries.

FIG. 1—Typical Buddha figure, seated in *dhyāna;* curly hair, but the *uṣṇṣa* is not preserved. Over life-size. C. third-fourth century A. D. Anurādhapura, Ceylon, *in situ.*

FIG. 2—Yakṣa. From Pārkham. Over life-size. (Cf. Fig. 47.) Usually assigned to the third century B. C. Mathurā Museum.

FIG. 3—Yakṣa. From Patna. Second century B. C. Indian Museum, Calcutta.

FIG. 4—Friar Bala's Bodhisattva (Buddha), made in Mathurā and set up at Sārnāth. Over life-size. (Cf. Figs. 18, 31.) Dated in the third year of Kaniṣka, i. e., 123 A. D. Sārnāth Museum.

FIG. 5—Buddha. From Mathurā. Typical Gupta example. Over life-size. (Cf. Fig. 33.) Mathurā Museum.

FIG. 6—Coin of Maues. Enlarged. (Gardner, *Coins of the Greek and Scythic Kings . . .*, XVII, 5.) C. 100 or 80 B. C.

FIG. 7—Coin of Azes. (Whitehead, *Cat. Coins Panjab Museum*, XI, 195.) C. 58 B. C.

FIG. 8—Coin of Kadapha (Kadphises I, c. 40-78 A. D.) Lahore Museum

FIG. 9—Ujjain coin, with seated Buddha on lotus, beside railed tree with *chatra*. Enlarged. (Cunningham, *Coins of Ancient India*, X, 10.) Probably first century, A. D.

FIG. 10—Coin of Kaniṣka, with seated Buddha. (Whitehead, *loc. cit.*, pl. XX, viii.) 120-165 A. D.

FIG. 11—Coin of Kaniṣka, with standing Buddha. (Gardner, *loc. cit.*, pl. XVII, 2.)

FIG. 12—Coin of Kaniṣka, with standing Buddha. British Museum.

FIG. 13—Kupiro Yakho (Kubera Yakṣa). From Bharhut. Early second century B. C. Indian Museum, Calcutta.

FIG. 14—Yakṣa with *caurī*, summit of north *toraṇa*. Sāñcī, *in situ*. C. 100 B. C.

FIG. 15—Indra as the Brahman Śānti. Bodhgayā, *in situ*. C. 100 B. C.

FIG. 16—Bodhisattva. From Mathurā. C. 100 A. D. Mathurā Museum.

FIG. 17—Bodhisattva Maitreya, Dhyāni Buddha in headdress, *amṛta* flask in left hand. From Mathurā. C. 100 A. D. Lucknow Museum.

FIG. 18—Buddha. From Mathurā. (Cf. Fig. 4.) C. 100 A. D. Lucknow Museum.

FIG. 19—The *Abhiniṣkramaṇa* of Buddha. 100-50 B. C. East *toraṇa*, front, middle architrave, Sāñcī, *in situ*.

FIG. 20—Buddha triad. C. 100 B. C. Three uprights between architraves of the north *toraṇa*, Sāñcī, *in situ*.

FIG. 21—The First Sermon in the Deer Park, Benares. Detail of a pediment from Mathurā. C. 100 A. D. Museum of Fine Arts, Boston.

FIG. 22—Detail from the same pediment; above, the Bowl-Relic on an altar with nimbus; below, the Bodhi-tree (Great Enlightenment of the Buddha).

FIG. 23—Sujātā approaching the Bodhi-tree, beneath which the Buddha is understood to be seated immediately prior to the Enlightenment. C. 100 B. C. Detail of middle architrave, north *toraṇa*, Sāñcī, *in situ*.

FIG. 24—Nāga standing under a tree. From railing, Pāṭaliputra. Third or early second century B. C. Indian Museum, Calcutta.

FIG. 25—Men seated in yoga pose, cross-legged, in the windows of an upper story. Early second century B. C. Railing medallion, from Bharhut. Indian Museum, Calcutta.

FIG. 26—The Nāga Erāpata worshipping the Buddha (represented by the Bodhi-tree and altar). Early second century B. C. Bharhut.

FIG. 27—Digha instructing his disciples. From the rail coping, Bharhut. Early second century B. C. Indian Museum, Calcutta.

FIG. 28—Stupa with worshippers; representing the *Parinirvāṇa* of the Buddha. Early second century B. C. Bharhut.

FIG. 29—*Vessantara Jātaka:* Gift of the Elephant. From the rail coping, Bharhut. Early second century B. C. Indian Museum, Calcutta.

FIG. 30—Head of Buddha. From Gandhāra. Early second century A. D. (?) Museum of Fine Arts, Boston.

FIG. 31—Head of Buddha. From Mathurā. Early second century A. D. Museum of Fine Arts, Boston.

FIG. 32—Head of Bodhisattva, probably Maitreya, with Dhyāni Buddha in headdress. From Gandhāra. Early second century A. D. Field Museum, Chicago.

FIG. 33—Head of Buddha, typical Gupta type. From Mathurā. Fifth century A. D. Museum of Fine Arts, Boston.

FIG. 34—Bodhisattva (so called in inscription). From Kaṭrā mound, Mathurā. Early second century A. D. Mathurā Museum.

FIG. 35—Buddha, similar to the last. Museum of Fine Arts, Boston.

FIG. 36—Bodhisattva Maitreya, with *amṛta* flask in left hand. Detail of pediment, Mathurā. C. 100 A. D. (?) Mathurā Museum.

FIG. 37—Seated Buddha or Bodhisattva with turban. From Mathurā. Second century A. D. Property of Messrs. Yamanaka.

FIG. 38—Above, the Buddha teaching; below, the Great First Meditation Detail of same pediment as Fig. 36.

FIG. 39—Seated Buddha or Bodhisattva, similar to Figs. 34, 35, and 38 above. From Mathurā. Early second century A. D. Mathurā Museum.

FIG. 40—The visit of Indra to the Buddha in the Indra-sāla guhā; on the upper right, the Yakṣa Vajrapāṇi, below, with mitre-like crown, Indra. From Mathurā. Second century A. D. Present location unknown; formerly the property of L. Rosenberg, Paris.

FIG. 41—*Ayāgapaṭa*, with seated Jina in center, attended by two Yakṣas. From Mathurā. Late first century A. D. (?) Lucknow Museum.

FIG. 42—Another *āyāgapaṭa*, in the center a seated Jina without attendants. Same source and present location.

FIG. 43—The Jina Pārśvanātha. From Mathurā. C. 100 A. D. (?) Mathurā Museum.

FIG. 44—Sūrya, the Sun-god, winged, with nimbus, in a chariot drawn by four horses. From Mathurā. First century A. D. (?) Mathurā Museum.

FIG. 45—Yakṣa with a purse, probably Kuvera. From Achnagar, near Mathurā. Second or third century A. D. Present location unknown.

FIG. 46—Nāga with two attendants supported by *makaras*. From railing pillar, Amarāvatī. Late second century A. D. Madras Museum.

FIG. 47—Yakṣa, Deoriyā, Allahābād. The deity wears a turban, and has a chatra over his head. (Cf. Fig. 18.) Third century B. C.

FIG. 48—Bodhisattva Maitreya, with the *amṛta* flask in the left hand. (Cf. Fig. 49.) First century A. D. (?) Timken (Burnet) Collection, New York.

FIG. 49—Nāga, with a flask in the left hand. (Cf. Fig. 48, and also *A. S. I.*, *A. R.*, 1919-20, pl. XXI, b, the same type seated, mediaeval, called Nāgārjuna, but in Vogel, *Indian Serpent Lore*, pl. XIV, designated a Nāga. Cf. also the Nāga Dadhikarṇa with a flask, *A. S. I.*, *A. R.*, 1924-5, pl. XL, a.) First century A. D. (?) Author's collection.

FIG. 50—Bodhisattva. From Mathurā. Early second century A. D. (?) University Museum, Philadelphia.

FIG. 51—Buddha. From Mathurā. Second century A. D. Present location unknown.

FIG. 52—Buddha. From Mathurā. Third century A. D. Present location unknown.

FIG. 53—Buddha. From Gandhāra. C. 100 A. D. (?)

FIG. 54—Buddha. From Gandhāra. C. 100 A. D.

FIG. 55—Bodhisattva. From Gandhāra (Sahr-i-Bahlol). C. 100 A. D. (?)

FIG. 56—Reliquary of Kaniṣka. From Peshāwar. Second quarter of second century A. D. Calcutta Museum.

FIG. 57—*Vessantara Jātaka.* From Gandhāra. (Cf. Fig. 29.) Second or third century A. D. Museum of Fine Arts, Boston.

FIG. 58—Six scenes from the life of the Buddha. From Mathurā. (This and the next show some Gandhāra features.) Second century A. D. Mathurā Museum.

FIG. 59—Two scenes from the life of the Buddha. From Mathurā. Second century A. D. Mathurā Museum.

FIG. 60—Seated Buddha, with two attendant caurī-bearers (Yakṣas). School of Amarāvatī. About 200 A. D. Field Museum, Chicago.

FIG. 61—Buddha. From Māṅkuwāṛ. Inscription dated equivalent to 448/9 A. D.

FIG. 62—Buddha. From Mathurā. Late second century A. D. (?) Sāñcī, *in situ.*

FIG. 63—Buddha. Fifth century A. D. Sāñcī, *in situ.*

FIG. 64—Jina with two Yakṣa attendants. Mediaeval. Mathurā Museum.

FIG. 65—The Bodhisattva Vajrapāṇi, copper. From Ceylon. Ninth century. Museum of Fine Arts, Boston.

FIG. 66—Buddha, copper, Nepal. C. tenth century. Museum of Fine Arts, Boston.

FIG. 67—The Jina Pārśvanātha, bronze, Kannaḍa. Mediaeval. Kay collection, Madras.

FIG. 68—Buddha. From Dong Duong, Annam, possibly of Indian or Sinhalese manufacture. C. third century A. D. Hanoi Museum.

FIG. 69—Buddha. From Mathurā. Third century A. D. Mathurā Museum.

FIG. 70—Buddha. From Anurādhapura, Ceylon. Third or fourth century A. D. Colombo Museum.

FIG. 71—Buddha. Said to have been found in Burma, but probably of Indian manufacture. C. sixth century A. D. Museum of Fine Arts, Boston.

FIG. 72—Buddha. From Sārnāth. C. fifth century A. D. Sārnāth Museum.

FIG. 73—Bodhisattva Padmapāṇi. From Sārnāth. C. fifth century A. D. Sārnāth Museum.

APPENDIX

As remarked by Kern (*Manual of Indian Buddhism*, p. 94), "There is no lack of legends anent the origin of Buddha images, but it would be difficult to discover in those tales, which are wholly discordant, something like a historical nucleus. Nothing definite results from the legends, except the fact that images of the Tathāgata were venerated by the faithful at the time of the tales being invented." The stories are well known. Most of the references will be found in Kern, *loc. cit.*, p. 94; see also J. Hackin, *Illustrations tibétaines d'une légende du Divyāvadāna*, in *Ann. du Musée Guimet*, *Bib. de Vulg.*, XL, 1914. I have not thought it worth while to cite any of these stories above. But there are some which are of considerable interest in connection with what has been said about the lay origin of the cult, the analogy with images of other deities in current use, and the hesitation with which a Buddha image was at first accepted as orthodox. The citations below are of interest as illustrating the psychology of those whose devotional feelings led to the use of Buddha images.

The *Mahāvaṁsa*, V, 90 ff., written no doubt when images were already well known, very naturally ascribes to Aśoka a desire to behold the likeness of Buddha. " 'Let us behold,' he is made to say, 'the form of the omiscient Great Sage, of him who hath boundless knowledge, who hath set rolling the Wheel of the True Doctrine.' " Then a Nāga king in response to this expressed desire "created a beauteous figure of the Buddha, endowed with the thirty-two greater signs and brilliant with the eighty lesser signs, surrounded by the fathom-long rays of glory and adorned with the crown of flames."

In the *Divyāvadāna*, ch. LXXVII, Upagupta compels Māra to exhibit himself in the shape of Buddha. Upagupta bows down to the form thus produced, and Māra is shocked at this apparent worship of himself and protests. Upagupta explains that he is adoring not Māra, but the person represented, "just as people venerating earthen images of gods do not revere the clay but the immortal ones represented by them. . . ."

"Indeed, I am well aware of this, that the foremost of teachers has passed away into Nirvāṇa, yet beholding his lovely likeness (*nayanakāntāṁ ākṛtiṁ*), I have bowed to that Rsi; it is not you whom I worship."

Analogous to the coming into use of a Buddha icon is the first use of the Buddha legend as material for a drama. In this connection the Kah-gyur (Schiefner, *Tibetan Tales*, no. XIII) has a story about an actor, who went first to the Nāga Nanda, a faithful worshipper of the Buddha (in whose lifetime the events are supposed to have taken place), to obtain from him the necessary data for the drama. Nanda, on hearing the purpose for which the information was required, refused contemptuously: "Wretched man," he said, "do you wish us to portray the Teacher for you? begone, for I will tell you nothing." The actor, however, obtained the required information from a learned nun and composed his drama. "He pitched a booth in Rājagṛha on the day when the festival of the Nāgarājas Girika and Sundara was celebrated and sounded a drum. And when a great crowd had collected, he exhibited in a drama . . . events in the life of Bhagavant, in harmony with the Abhiniṣkramaṇa Sūtra. Thereby the performers and the assembled crowds were confirmed in the faith. And they uttered sounds of approval, and he made a large profit."

All this must have been very like what took place when Buddha images first came into use. Incidentally it has some value for the history of the Indian drama.

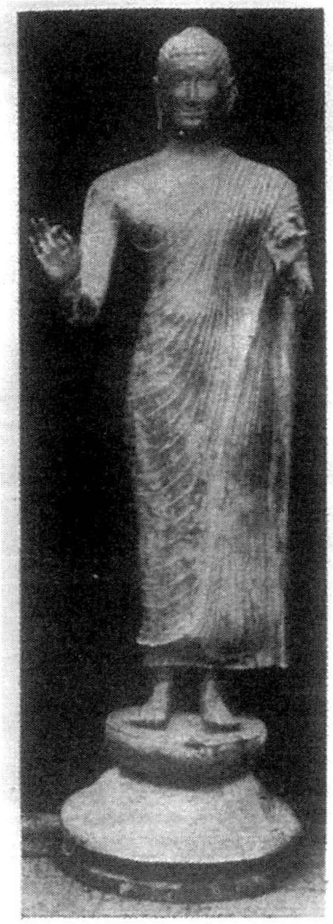

68—Buddha (*Annam*)

69—Buddha (*Mathurā*)

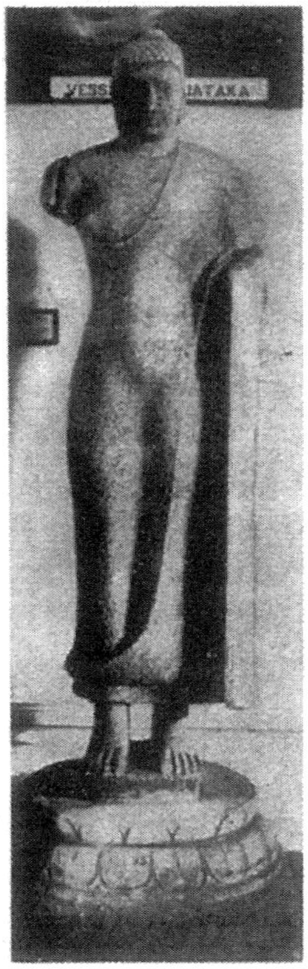

70—Buddha (*Ceylon*)

71—Buddha "*Burma*"

72—Buddha (*Sārnāth*)

73—Bodhisattva Padmapāṇi (*Sārnāth*)

Late Kuṣāna and Gupta Buddhas and Bodhisattvas